New Media, Campaigning and the 2008 Facebook Election

Some political observers dubbed the 2008 presidential campaign as "the Facebook Election". Barack Obama, in particular, employed social media such as blogs, Twitter, Flickr, Digg, YouTube, MySpace and Facebook to run a "grassroots-style" campaign. The Obama campaign was keenly aware that voters, particularly the young, are not simply consumers of information, but conduits of information as well. They often replaced the professional filter of traditional media with a social one. Social media allowed candidates to do electronically what previously had to be done through shoe leather and phone banks: contact volunteers and donors, and schedule and promote events. The 2008 Election marked a new era where the candidates no longer had complete control over their campaign message. The individual viewer in a campaign crowd with a cell phone can record a candidate's gaffe, post it on YouTube or Flickr and within days millions will be gasping or guffawing. The traditional campaign, with its centralized power and planning, although not dead, now coexists with an unstructured digital democracy. *New Media, Campaigning and the 2008 Facebook Election* examines the way social media changed how candidates campaigned, how the media covered the election and how voters received information.

This book is based on a special issue of *Mass Communication & Society*.

Thomas J. Johnson is the Amon G. Carter, Jr. Centennial Professor in the School of Journalism at the University of Texas at Austin, USA. He has studied the role of new media in the presidential election since 1992 and has authored more than 50 articles and book chapters, primarily in the area of political communication. Previous publications include *International Media Communication in a Global Age* (2009).

David D. Perlmutter is Director of the School of Journalism and Mass Communication and a Professor and Starch Faculty Fellow at The University of Iowa, USA. He is the author or editor of seven books on political communication including *Blogwars: The New Political Battleground* (2008). He has also written several dozen research articles for academic journals as well as more than 200 essays for US and international newspapers and magazines.

New Media, Campaigning and the 2008 Facebook Election

Edited by
Thomas J. Johnson and
David D. Perlmutter

Routledge
Taylor & Francis Group
LONDON AND NEW YORK

First published 2011
by Routledge
2 Park Square, Milton Park, Abingdon, Oxon, OX14 4RN

Simultaneously published in the USA and Canada
by Routledge
711 Third Avenue, New York, NY 10017

Routledge is an imprint of the Taylor & Francis Group, an informa business

British Library Cataloguing in Publication Data
A catalogue record for this book is available from the British Library

ISBN13: 978-0-415-67393-8

Typeset in Times New Roman
by Taylor & Francis Books

Disclaimer
The publisher would like to make readers aware that the chapters in this book are referred to as articles as they had been in the special issue. The publisher accepts responsibility for any inconsistencies that may have arisen in the course of preparing this volume for print.

MIX
Paper from
responsible sources
FSC
www.fsc.org   FSC® C004839

Printed and bound in Great Britain by the MPG Books Group

Contents

Notes on contributors   vii

1. Introduction: The Facebook Election
   Thomas J. Johnson and David D. Perlmutter   1

2. Intermedia Agenda-Setting and Political Activism: MoveOn.org
   and the 2008 Presidential Election
   Matthew W. Ragas and Spiro Kiousis   7

3. The 2008 Presidential Campaign: Political Cynicism in the Age of
   Facebook, MySpace and YouTube
   Gary Hanson, Paul Michael Haridakis, Audrey Wagstaff Cunningham,
   Rekha Sharma, and J. D. Ponder   31

4. Did Social Media Really Matter? College Students' Use of Online
   Media and Political Decision Making in the 2008 Election
   Matthew James Kushin and Masahiro Yamamoto   55

5. The 2008 Presidential Election, 2.0: A Content Analysis of
   User-Generated Political Facebook Groups
   Julia K. Woolley, Anthony M. Limperos and Mary Beth Oliver   79

6. The Writing on the Wall: A Content Analysis of College Students'
   Facebook Groups for the 2008 Presidential Election
   Juliana Fernandes, Magda Giurcanu, Kevin W. Bowers
   and Jeffrey C. Neely   101

Index   125

Notes on contributors

Kevin W. Bowers is a Ph.D. candidate in the College of Journalism and Communications, University of Florida. His research interests include uses of social networks and virtual worlds for educational purposes.

Audrey Wagstaff Cunningham is Instructor in the Department of Communication at Hiram College and a Doctoral Candidate in the School of Communication Studies at Kent State University.

Juliana Fernandes is an Assistant Professor in the School of Journalism and Mass Communication, Florida International University. Her research interests include political communication, affective impact of advertising, and effects of time perspective on voting behavior.

Magda Giurcanu is a Ph.D. candidate in the Department of Political Science, University of Florida. Her research interests include European electoral behavior, political communications, and party institutionalization in post-communist states.

Gary Hanson is Associate Professor in the School of Journalism & Mass Communication at Kent State University. His research interests include new media, politics and journalism ethics and accuracy.

Paul Michael Haridakis is Professor in the School of Communication Studies at Kent State University. His research interests include media uses and effects, new communication technologies, freedom of expression and media history.

Thomas J. Johnson is the Amon G. Carter, Jr. Centennial Professor in the School of Journalism at the University of Texas at Austin, USA. He has studied the role of new media in the presidential election since 1992 and has authored more than 50 articles and book chapters, primarily in the area of political communication. Previous publications include *International Media Communication in a Global Age* (2009).

Spiro Kiousis is Professor and Chair in the Department of Public Relations at University of Florida. His research interests include political public relations.

Matthew James Kushin is Assistant Professor in the Department of Communication at Utah Valley University. His research interests include political campaigns, online media, and social media.

Anthony M. Limperos is a Doctoral Candidate in the College of Communications at The Pennsylvania State University. His research interests include media uses and effects and new communication technology.

Jeffrey C. Neely is a Ph.D. candidate in the College of Journalism and Communications, University of Florida. His research interests include the role of youth voice in digital communications, community building, and media ethics.

Mary Beth Oliver is Distinguished Professor in the Department of Film=Video & Media Studies and is Co-Director of the Media Effects Research Lab in communications at The Pennsylvania State University. Her research interests include media effects, with a focus on media and emotion, and media and social cognition.

David D. Perlmutter is Director of the School of Journalism and Mass Communication and a Professor and Starch Faculty Fellow at The University of Iowa, USA. He is the author or editor of seven books on political communication including *Blogwars: The New Political Battleground* (2008). He has also written several dozen research articles for academic journals as well as more than 200 essays for US and international newspapers and magazines.

J. D. Ponder is a Doctoral Candidate in the School of Communication Studies at Kent State University.

Matthew W. Ragas is Assistant Professor in College of Communication at DePaul University. His research focuses on corporate and political communication.

Rekha Sharma is a Doctoral Candidate in the School of Communication Studies at Kent State University. Her research interests include political communication in news and popular culture as well as the uses and effects of media related to government conspiracy theories.

Julia K. Woolley is a Doctoral Candidate in the College of Communications at The Pennsylvania State University. Her research interests include media effects, entertainment psychology, and communication and new media.

Masahiro Yamamoto is a Doctoral Candidate in The Edward R. Murrow College of Communication at Washington State University. His research interests include online media, mass media and social organization, and public health.

Introduction: The Facebook Election

Thomas J. Johnson

Amon G. Carter Jr. Centennial Professor
University of Texas at Austin

David D. Perlmutter, Ph.D.

Director of the School of Journalism and
Mass Communication
Professor & Starch Faculty Fellow
College of Liberal Arts & Sciences
The University of Iowa

Introduction: The Facebook Election

During the race for the presidency in 2007–2008, one of the editors of this book, based on a November 2010 special issue of *Mass Communication & Society,* spent a month reading Barack Obama's official campaign MySpace page (Perlmutter, 2008). Its most notable feature was the posting of comments by thousands of people, not all of them supporters of the Illinois senator's bid for the White House. One of the most striking characteristics of at least some of the comments, which included text and a signature picture file representing the commenter, was their prurient, non-sequitur, and sometimes zany content. One commenter, presumably a young lady, employed a picture of a naked, buttocks-forward, and undulating woman accompanied by text passionately declaring her loyalty to the campaign. Others had cartoon figures in semidress and possible sexual distress; still more included creepy "wanted poster" images and accusations.

Anyone the least bit familiar with the rough-and-tumble world of social media will not be surprised that such weirdness and absurdity erupted front and center on an essentially open website. But the Obama MySpace page, in allowing—albeit briefly—such postings signaled a sea change in at least one way that organized political machines viewed the content that was published in their name and under their banner. Until well into the Internet era, political campaigns were all about message discipline and message control (Perlmutter, 1999; Stromer-Galley, 2000). Since paid media were horrendously expensive, political communication victory for a campaign was measured by the mainstream media picking up of the designed infobyte or visbyte of the day. Control over all content, from bumper stickers to radio ads, was centralized, with only a few power players typically consisting of consultants, managers, and the candidate (and his or her spouse). Many critics inside and outside of the political-journalism industrial complex complained that there was no democracy in democratic politics.

The 2003–2004 Howard Dean campaign, with his reliance on Blog for America, served as a 1.0 prototype, and Obama 2007–2008 as a 2.0 successful model, have proved that politics as we know it has changed in a fundamental way. Immediately, of course, we must put limitations and offer contexts to such a sweeping conclusion. First, over the history of the introduction of new communication technologies, there has always been a pushback by the old. Print newspapers railed against radio and then television as media unworthy of serious journalism. Second, Obama did not win the presidency because of Facebook. All commentators and insiders agree that his nomination campaign especially was a well-run traditional political machine that would have made a 1950s old pol proud. He "got out the vote" (GOTV) door-to-door as well as Tweeted. He gave great fundraising speeches as well as mobilized thousands of independent supporters to start up pro-Obama blogs to raise money and enthusiasm. He lined up union endorsements as well as texted thoughts of the day.

Nevertheless, we are in a new era where the candidates no longer have complete control over the message. The individual viewer in a campaign crowd with a cell phone can record a candidate's gaffe, post it on YouTube or Flickr and within days millions will be gasping or guffawing. Individuals can create their own blog to tout their views on the campaign or post those same messages on discussion boards, social media sites or Twitter. The traditional campaign, with its centralized power and planning, although not dead, now coexists—sometimes uneasily—with an unstructured digital democracy.

The Facebook election: New media and the 2008 election campaign

In this book political communication scholars examine the way in which Online Social-Interactive Media (OSIM), more specifically social network sites, blogs, micro-blogs (like Twitter), video-sharing sites, and online discussion forums, changed the ways candidates campaigned, how the media covered the election and how voters received information in the 2008 election changed the ways candidates campaigned, how the media covered the election and how voters received information in the 2008 election. We use the term "Online Social-Interactive Media" rather than social network sites to characterize social media examined in this book. As Boyd and Ellison's (2007) classic definition of social network sites indicates, these are sources that allow users to create profiles and establish online connections with friends and acquaintances. This definition characterizes social network sites such as Facebook and LinkedIn, but does not complete account for other social media sites such as micro-blogs (e.g., Twitter), video-sharing sites (e.g. Twitter) and online discussion forums. OSIMs refer to media that rely on what Bruns (2008) characterized as produsage, in which the boundaries between producers and consumers are eliminated so that users create content for each other in communities that rely on user collaboration and an ethic of openly sharing user creations.

While several of the chapters in this book address the question of what are social media sites, in chapter 4 Matthew J. Kushin and Masahiro Yamamoto examine the issue directly. The authors conducted a principle component analysis of 15 political items and five loaded on attention to social media: personal blogs, video-sharing websites, micro blogs, social network sites and online forums and discussion boards.

Four of the five chapters in this text centered on the user of OSIM with two examining content of user-generated Facebook groups and two examining the effects of OSIMs on citizens' attitudes and behaviors. The fifth chapter took a broader approach by examining intermedia agenda setting among activist media, activist citizens, and campaign ads produced by the Obama campaign and by MoveOn.org.

Past content analyses of social media pages tend to center on characteristics of the author of a social network page (Grasmuck, Martin, & Zhao, 2009) or candidates' social network profiles (Compton, 2007). Few have focused on users of Facebook groups.

Chapter 6 examines 562 wall posts from college Facebook groups devoted to Obama and McCain in seven battleground states to see how these groups facilitate political dialog and civic engagement through wall posts made by group members. The authors found that political discussion dominated the discussion between posters, as they used the Facebook groups to transmit important information related to the candidates' campaign, issues and appearances rather than for social purposes. The authors argue that the results bode well for the potential of social network sites to foster civic engagement among young voters.

In chapter 5, Julia Woolley, Anthony Limperos, and Mary Oliver examine the top four Facebook groups in terms of size and a systematic random sample of 129 other groups for each candidate. They discovered that, in line with major media reports, that groups focusing on Obama were more actively used and had a higher group membership than McCain-focused groups. Comments on Obama's groups were overwhelmingly positive, while for McCain comments were decidedly negative. While the other content analysis stressed the benefits of Facebook groups, the authors here feared that their results demonstrated that while the social network site provides a platform for individuals to express their beliefs, their expressions tended to be partisan and polarizing.

Just as the content analyses offered conflicting predictions about the benefits of OSIMs, so have studies that have explored effects of OSIMs on their audience. Studies suggest that *in general*, social network sites and blogs may not have much influence on political attitudes and behavior (Cozma & Postelnicu, 2008; Zhang, Johnson, Seltzer & Bichard, 2010), although political uses of SNS (Kim & Geidner 2008; Utz, 2009; Valenzuela, Park & Kee, 2009; Vitak et al., 2010) and blogs (Gil de Zuniga, Puig, & Rojas, 2009) may better predict political attitudes and behavior. Another study found that while You-Tube and social network sites both predicted both offline and online political participation, social network sites did a better job predicting other political measures (Johnson, Zhang, Bichard & Seltzer, 2010). Not surprisingly, then, the two studies in this issue that explored political effects of OSIMs reached different conclusions.

Chapter 3 examines the relationship between social network sites, video-sharing sites, political blogs and political cynicism. The authors found that while video-sharing sites and political blogs were unrelated to political cynicism, amount of time spent using social network sites for political information led to lowering of political cynicism. The authors suggested that the reason why SNS predicted lower political cynicism and blogs did not was the strong interpersonal nature of SNS. Two other social measures, the influence of one's family and friends as socializing agents and being motivated to use OSIMs for companionship, also were linked to lower levels of political cynicism.

In chapter 4, Matthew J. Kushin and Masahiro Yamamoto discovered that unfortunately, OSIMs matter little in terms of political efficacy and situational political involvement (i.e., attention, interest, seeking out and staying informed about elections). On the other hand, a behavior measure examining OSIMs, online expression (writing blog posts on political issues; creating and posting online audio, video, animation photos or computer artwork to express political views; sharing political news, video clips or others' blog posts online; and exchanging opinions about politics via e-mail, social network sites, micro blogging or instant messenger) did predict situational political involvement, but not political efficacy. The authors suggested their results reinforce studies examining the positive effects of online political discussion and that online expression may have proved a stronger predictor of involvement than attention to OSIMs because expression indicates stronger cognitive involvement.

In the final chapter in this volume, Matthew Ragas and Spiro Kiousis examine agenda setting in the OSIM environment. Researchers (e.g. Chaffee & Metzger, 2001) have questioned whether agenda setting can remain relevant in the Internet age. As the Internet has equaled newspapers as a source of information and people are getting information from a host of sources beyond traditional media, it no longer makes sense to talk about a *single* media agenda. Similarly, users have more information to choose from as well as more control over what sources they will search out, indicating that the public will increasingly have influence on the media agenda. Ragas and Kiousis demonstrate that agenda setting retains its relevancy in the OSIM world by examining intermedia agenda-setting effects among partisan news media coverage and political action groups, citizen activists and official campaign advertising on YouTube. The setting of their study was the political activist organization MoveOn.org's "Obama in 30 seconds" online ad contest during the 2008 primaries where they tested for the transfer of issue and attribute salience among political media content appearing in the partisan newsmagazine *The Nation*, YouTube ads created by the Obama campaign and by citizen activists in the MoveOn.org contest as well as ads designed by the activist organization. The strongest relationship was found between partisan media coverage and the "Obama in 30 seconds" ads, and significant relationships were also found between the MoveOn.org ads and citizen activist-created ads. Second-level agenda-setting effects were discovered between the Obama negative ads and the "Obama in 30 seconds" ads, as well as the Obama negative ads and the MoveOn.org ads. The results demonstrate that agenda setting is alive and well and can be extended to political activist communication efforts and consumer-generated content.

References

Boyd, D.M. & Ellison, N.B. (2007). Social network sites: Definition, history, and scholarship*Journal of Computer-Mediated Communication, 13(1),* article 11. http://jcmc.indiana.edu/vol13/issue1/boyd.ellison.html

Bruns, A. (2008). Blogs, Wikipedia, Second Life, and beyond: From production to produsage. New York: Peter Lang Publishing.

Chaffee, S.H, & Metzger, M. (2001). The end of mass communication? *Mass Communication & Society, 4,* 365-379.

Compton, J. (2008, November). *Mixing friends with politics: A functional analysis of '08 presidential candidates social networking profiles.* Paper presented at the annual meeting of the National Communication Association.

Correa, T., Hinsley, A.W., & Gil de Zuniga, J. (2010). Who interacts on the Web?: The intersection of users' personality and social media use. *Computers in Human Behavior, 26,* 47-253.

Cozma, R., & Postelnicu, M. (2008, August). *Political uses and perceived effects of campaigning on MySpace.* Paper presented at the annual conference of the Association for Education in Journalism & Mass Communication, Chicago, IL

Gil de Zuniga, H., Puig, E., & Rojas, H. (2009). Weblogs, traditional sources online and political participation: An assessment of how the Internet is changing the political environment. *New Media & Society, 11, 553-574.*

Grasmuck, S., Martin, J., & Zhao, S. (2009). Ethno-racial identity displays on Facebook. *Journal of Computer-Mediated Communication, 15,* 158-188.

Johnson, T.J., Zhang, W., Bichard, S. L., & Seltzer, T. (2010). United we stand? Online social network sites and civic engagement. In Z. Papacharissi (ed.). Networked Self: Identity, Community, and Culture on Social Network Sites (pp. 185-207). New York: Routledge.

Kim, Y.M., & Geidner, N. (2008, May). *Politics as friendship: The impact of online social networks on young voters' political behavior.* Paper presented at the annual convention of the International Communication Association, Montreal, Canada

Perlmutter, D.D. (2008). Blogwars: The new political battleground. New York: Oxford University Press, 2008.

Perlmutter, D.D. ed. (1999). Manship School Guide to Political Communication. Baton Rouge: LSU Press,1999.

Stromer-Galley, J. (2000) On-line interaction and why candidates avoid it. *Journal of Communication*, 50, 111-132.

Utz, S. (2009). The (potential) benefits of campaigning via social network sites. *Journal of Computer-Mediated Communication, 14,* 227-243.

Valenzuela, S., Park, N., & Kee, K.F. (2009). Is there social capital in a social network site?: Facebook use and college students' life satisfaction, trust and participation. *Journal of Computer-Mediated Communication, 14*, 875-901.

Vitak, J., Zube, P., Smock, A, Carr, C., Ellison, N., & Lampe, C. (In press). It's complicated: Facebook users' participation in the 2008 election. *CyberPyschology, Behavior, and Social Networking.*

Zhang, W., Johnson, T.J., Seltzer, T., & Bichard, S. (2010). The revolution will be networked: The influence of social network sites on political attitudes and behaviors. *Social Science Computer Review*, 28, 75-92.

Intermedia Agenda-Setting and Political Activism: MoveOn.org and the 2008 Presidential Election

Matthew W. Ragas
College of Communication
DePaul University

Spiro Kiousis
Department of Public Relations
University of Florida

This study tested for intermedia agenda-setting effects among explicitly partisan news media coverage and political activist group, citizen activist, and official campaign advertisements on YouTube—*all in support of the same candidate*. The setting for this investigation was the political activist organization MoveOn.org's "Obama in 30 Seconds" online ad contest, which was held during the 2008 U.S. presidential election primaries. The data provided evidence of first- and second-level agenda-setting relationships. Partial correlations revealed that the citizen activist issue agenda, as articulated in the contest ads, was most strongly related to the partisan media coverage, rather than to the issue priorities of the official Obama or MoveOn.org ads on YouTube. These results extend the intermedia agenda setting framework to political activist communication efforts and consumer-generated content.

One of the core objectives of political communication efforts, such as campaign advertising, is to increase the salience of political issues and candidates in news media coverage and in the mind of the public (Kiousis, Mitrook, Wu, & Seltzer, 2006). With its rich history in political campaign settings, agenda-setting theory has been used to assess the transfer of salience among the candidate, media, and public agendas (e.g., McCombs, 2005; McCombs & Shaw, 1993). A small body of work (e.g., Ghorpade, 1986; Golan, Kiousis, & McDaniel, 2007; Lopez-Escobar, Llamas, McCombs, & Lennon, 1998; Roberts & McCombs, 1994; Sweetser, Golan, & Wanta, 2008) has focused specifically on the agenda-setting effects of candidate political advertising. Missing from the literature is a simultaneous investigation of the intermedia agenda-setting relationships between news media coverage and political ads generated by a campaign, a political activist group, and citizen activists, all of which support *the same candidate*, during an election. Therefore, the purpose of this study is to build theory by testing for first- and second-level intermedia agenda-setting effects in the underexplored context of online political ads and explicitly partisan media coverage and to extend theory by incorporating ads generated by an activist group and citizen activists—not just official candidate ads—into this investigation.

The backdrop for this analysis is the "Obama in 30 Seconds" contest, which was held during the primary season in spring 2008 by the progressive group MoveOn.org, one of the largest Web-based political activist organizations in the world (Hayes, 2008; Price, 2004). MoveOn.org encouraged citizen activists to create online ads in support of Democrat presidential candidate Barack Obama. The contest received more than 1,000 ad submissions (A. Green, personal communication, May 12, 2008) and the winning ad aired on national television. This contest provides a unique setting for assessing intermedia agenda-setting effects among professional (Obama and MoveOn.org official YouTube ads) and citizen activist-created YouTube ads (Obama in 30 Seconds submissions), and an explicitly partisan news media outlet (the progressive political magazine *The Nation*), outside of the general election period.

LITERATURE REVIEW

First- and Second-Level Intermedia Agenda-Setting

More than 40 years ago, Bernard C. Cohen (1963) made the now-famous observation that the mass media may not tell the public "what to think" but it is stunningly successful in telling the public "what to think about"

(p. 13). The seminal Chapel Hill study conducted by McCombs and Shaw (1972) during the 1968 U.S. presidential election provided empirical support for Cohen's prognostication. This initial investigation of the agenda-setting hypothesis found that the mass media set the agenda of issues for the presidential campaign by influencing the salience of issues among voters (McCombs & Shaw, 1972). Over the ensuing decades since the publication of this initial study, several hundred subsequent investigations have supported the agenda-setting role of the news media on public opinion (McCombs, 2006). Although agenda-setting research has broadened its scope and focus over the years, its theoretical core has remained consistent: the transfer of salience from one agenda to another (McCombs, 2005; McCombs & Shaw, 1993; Weaver, 2007).

The core assertion in traditional agenda-setting research is that media attention to specific "objects" (e.g., issues, candidates, companies, activist groups, etc.) in the news leads to increased public concern with these same "objects." The transfer of object salience from one agenda to another has come to be known as "first-level" agenda-setting (Lopez-Escobar et al., 1998, McCombs, 2006). Agendas consist of not only a set of objects but the attributes that are chosen by communicators to describe and define these objects. Said another way, the media not only may tell the public "what to think about" (object salience) but also may influence "how to think about" (attribute salience) those objects. This transfer of attribute salience is identified as "second-level" agenda-setting (Lopez-Escobar et al., 1998, McCombs, 2006). Two different types of attributes have been identified in the literature: substantive and affective attributes (McCombs & Evatt, 1995; McCombs, Lopez-Escobar, & Llamas, 2000). Substantive attributes are the cognitive characteristics that describe objects in communication messages, whereas affective attributes refer to the valence dimension of attribute salience in messages (Coleman & Banning, 2006; Sheafer, 2007). For example, a negative political ad about the Iraq war, which emphasizes the U.S. casualties aspect of this issue, would exhibit issue salience (Iraq war), affective attribute salience (negative tone), and substantive attribute salience (casualties).

Moving beyond the media influence on the public agenda, intermedia agenda-setting examines how media content shapes other media content, including relationships among news media content and political advertisements (e.g., Ghorpade, 1986; Golan et al., 2007; Lopez-Escobar et al., 1998; Roberts & McCombs, 1994; Sweetser et al., 2008). The current study fits under what McCombs (1992) defined as the "fourth stage" of agenda-setting research, which includes intermedia agenda-setting, and more broadly seeks to better understand the various forces that build and shape the media agenda.

The Compelling-Arguments Hypothesis

An understudied aspect of agenda-setting is the compelling-arguments hypothesis (Ghanem, 1997; McCombs, 2006; McCombs & Ghanem, 2003). According to this proposition, the transfer of salience is not limited to a transfer of salience between objects and the attributes of objects on the source, media, and public agendas (Ghanem, 1997; McCombs, 2006; McCombs & Ghanem, 2003). The compelling-arguments hypothesis posits that when a particular attribute of an object is emphasized on one agenda, there may be a shift in the *overall salience* afforded that object on another agenda. In other words, compelling-arguments deals with the potential impact of attribute salience on object salience (Sheafer, 2007). According to McCombs (2006), "compelling arguments are frames...that enjoy high success among the public" (p. 92). He further asserted that, "certain characteristics of an object may resonate with the public in such a way that they become especially compelling arguments for the salience of the issue, person or topic under consideration" (McCombs, 2006, p. 92).

Several studies have explored the influence of affective and substantive compelling arguments. Although the compelling-arguments hypothesis had not yet been formally introduced, Schoenbach and Semetko (1992) found that the positive tone (affective attribute) with which a certain issue was covered by the news media *reduced* the perceived salience of the issue in the public mind. On the other hand, Sheafer (2007) found that negative tone in media coverage of the economy *increased* the perceived salience of the economy on the public agenda. A study by Yioutas and Segvic (2003) found that substantive attributes used by the news media served as compelling arguments to decrease the salience of the Clinton/Lewinsky scandal on the public agenda. In essence, the media's choice of attributes to describe the scandal, the object of interest in this study, diminished the public salience of the scandal (Yioutas & Segvic, 2003). Finally, research conducted by Kiousis (2005) across five U.S. presidential elections (1980–1996) provided modest evidence that media salience of presidential candidate attributes was positively associated with the perceived public salience of those candidates.

Based on a review of the compelling arguments literature, only one previous study has specifically analyzed the compelling-arguments hypothesis using political advertisements. In an investigation of candidate advertising, news content, and public opinion during the 2004 U.S. presidential campaign, Golan and colleagues (2007) predicted that the salience of the affective attributes of issues in candidate political ads would be positively related to the perceived salience of these same issues in public opinion. Although the Bush campaign ads did not support this hypothesis, a positive relationship was found for both the positive and negative Kerry ads (affective attributes) with public opinion. The current study builds on and extends the work of Golan et al. (2007) by testing for affective compelling arguments in political advertising created by a candidate's campaign as well as ads generated by a political activist group and citizen activists.

Agenda-Setting and Political Advertising

A body of work has emerged over the years specifically focused on evaluating the agenda-setting function of advertising, primarily in the context of campaign advertisements during election contests. For example, research by Bowers (1973) found a significant association between the agenda of issues reflected in public opinion polls and candidate newspaper ads for several senatorial and gubernatorial contests. An investigation by Atkin and Heald (1976) revealed a moderate association between voters' knowledge of issue positions by the candidates and exposure to radio and television ads. Research into the agenda-setting function of advertising appeared dormant for several years until this perspective drew the attention of advertising scholars Sutherland and Galloway (1981). According to Sutherland and Galloway (1981), "the main implication of agenda-setting theory is that the major goal of advertising may be to focus consumers' attention on what values, products, brands, or attributes to think about rather than to try to persuade consumers what to think of these" (p. 26).

Although Sutherland and Galloway (1981) concluded that the agenda-setting function of advertising *was* worth exploring further, this notion was not empirically tested again until Ghorpade (1986) analyzed the agenda-setting function of political ads during the 1984 North Carolina senatorial campaign between Jesse Helms and Jim Hunt. This study found a transfer of issue salience from both television news and candidate advertising to the public agenda of issues, although there was not a significant association between the television news coverage and the candidate advertising agendas. Using the 1990 Texas gubernatorial campaign as its backdrop, Roberts and McCombs (1994) found that the salience of issues in televised political advertising influenced both newspaper and television news coverage of the issues.

Research by Lopez-Escobar and colleagues (1998) replicated the aforementioned Roberts and McCombs study and extended this work to explore for second-level agenda-setting effects in political ads during the 1995 regional elections in Spain. Lopez-Escobar and colleagues found that the substantive attribute agenda in newspaper political ads influenced both the newspaper and television news agendas. In addition, the Lopez-Escobar et al. study found that television news coverage influenced the agenda of substantive attributes in televised political ads. A study by Boyle (2001) on intermedia agenda-setting effects during the 1996 U.S. presidential election revealed that televised political ads from the major party candidates influenced media coverage.

More recently, Golan and colleagues (2007) uncovered mixed evidence of first- and second-level agenda-setting effects from political ads during the 2004 U.S. presidential election. At the first level, there was a significant relationship between the issue agenda of Kerry ads and media coverage. The Bush ad agenda was not significantly associated with coverage. At the second level, a significant relationship was found between the Kerry negative ads and public opinion. As with the first-level findings, the positive and negative Bush ads were not significantly linked with public opinion. Conversely, recent research by Sweetser et al. (2008) examining candidate ads and candidate blogs during the 2004 U.S. presidential election concluded that the ads did *not* impact the salience of issues in media coverage. The study did find evidence of a significant linkage between the salience of issues on candidate blogs and media coverage (Sweetser et al., 2008).

Agenda-Setting and Activist Groups

In a multidisciplinary review of scholarship on the role and influence of advocacy organizations, including political activist groups, in the U.S. political process, Andrews and Edwards (2004) identified agenda-setting as a goal of these organizations. Specifically, they asserted that "the mass media and public opinion are important venues for gauging the influence of advocacy organizations on the public agenda" (p. 493). According to these researchers, advocacy and activist organizations attempt to raise the salience of their issues and concerns through demonstrations, education campaigns, and lobbying efforts (Andrews & Edwards, 2004). Although highlighting that these organizations attempt to set the agenda of the media and the public, this review lacks discussion on the use of advertising campaigns by these groups to shape issue priorities.

Although agenda-setting scholarship to date has lacked analysis specifically involving *political activist* advertising efforts, the literature is sprinkled with discussions of agenda-setting by activist groups in largely nonelection settings. For example, Carpenter (2007) studied how and why advocates and transnational advocacy networks pay attention to certain issues and not to others. Research by Hicks (2004) explored how the European Union influenced the social movement agendas of environmental activists in Poland, Hungary, and the Czech Republic. Using the backdrop of Royal Dutch/Shell and its policies in Nigeria in 1995, a study by Holzer (2007) found that local activists successfully pressured this multinational firm by influencing the media and public agendas in Western countries. Similarly,

Pralle (2006a, 2006b) found evidence of the communication efforts of anti-pesticide advocacy groups having an effect on the public policy agenda on this issue.

Two recent studies have explored the use of the Internet by activists for communicating their political agendas. Kim (2006) analyzed how civic groups in South Korea in 2000 and 2004 engineered a "blacklisting campaign" to defeat politicians who were deemed to be incompetent or antireform. The "agenda-setting prominence" that was achieved by this "blacklisting" alliance was in large part due to its very effective use of the Internet in publicizing its platform and organizing its supporters (Kim, 2006, p. 519). Schiffer (2006) studied a less successful use of the Internet by blogger activists during the Downing Street Memo controversy. Blogger activists had little success in impacting the news media agenda but did succeed in influencing the op-ed pages of major newspapers for a short period (Schiffer, 2006). Based on this review, the current study represents one of the first investigations from an agenda-setting perspective into ads generated by a Web-based activist group during an election.

Online Political Activists and Young News Consumers

The emergence and use of new communication technologies such as the Internet has been credited with creating "a sea change" in the practice of social and political activism on a global basis (de Jong, Shaw, & Stammers, 2005, p. 7). The Web provides powerful new opportunities for organization and collaboration among fellow activists as well as new ways to effectively distribute messages to supporters, the public, and the media. Over the past decade, a diverse range of activist-driven issue campaigns have benefited from using Web-based communication tools, such as social networking Web sites, blogs, e-mail newsletters, online petitions, electronic bulletin boards, and virtual sit-ins (de Jong et al., 2005; McCaughey & Ayers, 2003). The widespread adoption of broadband connections has resulted in Web video platforms, such as YouTube, becoming a viable new communication option for activists.

Survey research by Pew Internet & American Life Project (2007) has sketched a profile of online political activists in the U.S. According to Pew, "this is a population disproportionately weighted towards the young, the relatively well educated, and the well-to-do" that is "dominated by those who have broadband connections" (p. 17). These activists are more likely to be liberal than conservative and are heavy consumers of news in all forms. They are more likely than others to seek out nonmainstream news sources and media outlets that share their point of view. They also exhibit the most aggressive use of the Web to do various political activities, such as watching politics-related Web video clips. Although not specifically focused on online political activists, a two-site study by Coleman and McCombs (2007) found that media agenda-setting effects were only slightly weaker with the younger generation (18- to 34-year-olds) than with two older generations (Baby Boomers and the Civic Generation).

MoveOn.org and "Obama in 30 Seconds"

With more than 3 million members, the progressive group MoveOn.org is one of the largest, and most well-known, Web-based political activist organizations in the world (Hayes, 2008; Price, 2004). MoveOn.org has been acknowledged as pioneering "the use of e-mail and Web technologies as creative tools to further its political agenda" (Solomon, 2005, p. 9). In particular, MoveOn.org has been credited for using controversial advertising to reshape the media battlefield (Babbin, 2007) and influence Democratic politics (Herszenhorn, 2007). For example, in 2007, MoveOn.org ran a full-page ad in the *New York Times* titled "General Petraeus or General Betray Us," which questioned the credibility of General David Petraeus, the American commander in Iraq (Herszenhorn, 2007). MoveOn.org seems to realize its agenda-setting potential, as evidenced by a spring 2008 e-mail sent by Nita Chaudhary, Campaign Director at MoveOn.org, in which she asked supporters for funds to place a new commercial "on the air" and "get the media talking" (N. Chaudhary, personal communication, April 30, 2008).

For the first time in its 10-year history, MoveOn.org endorsed a presidential candidate, Democratic senator Barack Obama, for president in the 2008 election (Zeleny & Healy, 2008). As part of encouraging grass roots support for Obama, MoveOn.org held a contest in the spring of 2008 called Obama in 30 Seconds (http://www.obamain30seconds.org) in which it encouraged citizen activists to make YouTube ads about him. The contest received more than 1,000 ad submissions and millions of YouTube.com views (A. Green, personal communication, May 12, 2008). More than 5.5 million votes were cast in deciding the finalists for the contest (A. Green, personal communication, May 12, 2008). The winning ad, Obamacan, was aired by MoveOn.org on national television.

Hypotheses and Research Questions

Based on the logic of first-level intermedia agenda-setting, the following hypotheses are submitted:

H1: The salience of issues in MoveOn.org ads will be positively associated with the salience of issues in Obama in 30 Seconds ads.

H2: The salience of issues in Obama campaign ads will be positively associated with the salience of issues in Obama in 30 Seconds ads.

H3: The salience of issues in MoveOn.org ads will be positively associated with the salience of issues in Obama campaign ads.

H4: The salience of issues in the ads will be positively associated with the salience of issues in the progressive media coverage.

Based on the logic of second-level intermedia agenda-setting, the following hypotheses and research question are submitted:

H5: The salience of affective attributes in MoveOn.org ads will be positively associated with the salience of issues in Obama in 30 Seconds ads.

H6: The salience of affective attributes in Obama campaign ads will be positively associated with the salience of issues in Obama in 30 Seconds ads.

H7: The salience of affective attributes in Obama campaign ads will be positively associated with the salience of issues in MoveOn.org ads.

RQ1: Will the MoveOn.org ads, Obama ads or progressive media coverage be the most strongly associated with the Obama in 30 Seconds ads regarding the salience of issues?

METHOD

This study consisted of four separate content analyses of political ads and news media content during the heart of the primary period leading up to the 2008 U.S. presidential election. A total of 186 ads were collected and analyzed to determine the three ad agendas endorsing Obama (MoveOn.org, Obama in 30 Seconds, Obama campaign), and 369 news stories were collected and analyzed to provide a proxy for the explicitly progressive news media agenda (*The Nation*). The purpose of this study is to test for first- and second-level intermedia agenda-setting associations among news media content and professional and citizen activist-created political ads—all in support of the same candidate—outside of the general election period. Ads and news stories were examined to determine the salience of issues and attributes for each agenda. Each ad and news story served as the unit of analysis.

Selection of Sample

The sample period for the media agenda and the Obama campaign and MoveOn.org ad agendas ran from June 27, 2007, the date which the first

Obama ad was added to the candidate's official YouTube channel, through March 26, 2008, the day before the Obama in 30 Seconds ad contest began. By late March the majority of states had held their primaries or caucuses. The 9-month sample period selected for this study is similar in length to the 8-month time frame selected by two recent agenda-setting studies involving political ads (e.g., Golan et al., 2007; Sweetser et al., 2008). The submission period for MoveOn.org's Obama in 30 Seconds ad contest started March 27 and ended April 15.

All Obama campaign and MoveOn.org video ads that were identified as having been added to their official YouTube channels within the period of June 27 to March 26 were manually downloaded for analysis. This process resulted in 37 MoveOn.org ads and 48 Obama ads, which comprise the body of content for determining this study's MoveOn.org and Obama ad agendas, respectively.

The citizen activist-created ads for the Obama in 30 Seconds contest were displayed on the ObamaIn30Seconds.org Web site. The ads were shown one at a time on a random basis to site visitors. Once an ad had been voted on, another ad would then be displayed. The investigators manually downloaded 906 citizen activist-created ads from the contest site. According to MoveOn.org, the contest received greater than 1,000 submissions in total. Using a systematic random sampling technique (starting from a random point within the ads that were collected and then selecting every 9th ad in this sample), 101 of these ads were selected to form the subsample that was then analyzed to determine the citizen activist ad agenda. This subsample size is consistent with recent agenda-setting scholarship involving ads (e.g., Golan et al., 2007; Sweetser et al., 2008).

The Nation, self-described as "the flagship of the Left," was selected as the proxy for the progressive news media coverage because it is the largest explicitly progressive political news and opinion magazine in the United States (Amazon.com, 2009). The explicitly conservative equivalents to *The Nation* are *The Weekly Standard* and *National Review*. The 33 issues of *The Nation* that were published during the 9-month sample period were manually downloaded from the magazine's digital archive for analysis. All hard news stories were included in the sample. This process resulted in 369 news stories, which comprise the body of content for determining the progressive media agenda.

Content and Coding

For each of the four content analyses that were conducted, ads and news stories were probed to determine the agenda of issues. The Obama campaign and MoveOn.org ads also were probed to determine their respective agendas of affective attributes. Given that MoveOn.org instructed Obama in 30 Second contest ad submissions to be *positive* in tone, the citizen activist-created ads were not coded for affective attributes. Consistent with prior agenda-setting scholarship, salience was determined by the frequency of issue and attribute mentions in the content analyzed (e.g., Kiousis, 2005; Miller, Andsager, & Reichert, 1998; Tedesco, 2001). Each ad and news story served as the unit of analysis, and an ad and news story could be coded for the presence of multiple issues and their respective affective attributes.

To determine issue salience, each ad and news story was coded for the presence (1) or absence (0) of the political issues that are outlined next. To determine affective attribute salience, when a political issue was present in an ad, the corresponding affective attribute was coded for negative (1), neutral (2), or positive (3) tone. This two-level coding system allows for a test of first-level relationships, as well as a test of the previously discussed compelling-arguments hypothesis of second-level agenda-setting (Ghanem, 1997; McCombs, 2006; McCombs & Ghanem, 2003). Given that this study tests for affective compelling arguments, the content was not also coded for substantive attributes.

The political issues monitored were the economy, Iraq war, energy/fuel, health care, jobs, fix government, education, environment, and taxes. Consistent with previous agenda-setting research, these issues were selected based on a careful preliminary review of public opinion polls rating the most important campaign issues during the time frame of the study. The selection of nine political issues for analysis is within the range of the number of issues used in previous studies testing for agenda-setting effects from political ads (e.g., Ghorpade, 1986; Golan et al., 2007; Lopez-Escobar et al., 1998; Roberts & McCombs, 1994; Sweetser et al., 2008). Ads and news stories were also coded for the relevant descriptive information, such as the date, source, and ad or story title. The stories were also coded for whether they were an article, column, or editorial.

Intercoder Reliability

A randomly selected subsample of ads (20% of the total) was analyzed by a second trained coder to assess reliability. Intercoder reliability for issue salience was .97 using Holsti's (1969) formula and .90 using Scott's pi (1955). The latter formula is especially rigorous as it corrects for chance agreement. The reliability figures for the affective attributes in the ads were .94 and .84. Based on a randomly selected subsample of news articles (10% of the total), intercoder reliability for issue salience was .96 using Holsti's (1969) calculation and .87 using Scott's pi.

Data Analysis Strategy

Spearman's rho correlations (e.g., McCombs & Bell, 1996; McCombs & Shaw, 1972) and partial correlations were the statistical tests utilized for comparing the agendas regarding issue and attribute salience. Because this is an exploratory study, this approach is appropriate for identifying relationships among the agendas. However, these correlations do not prove causality and represent only an opening gambit of evidence for an intermedia agenda-setting effect among these various actors. The appearance of significant correlations in this study would lay the groundwork for future research that looks at potential causal relationships, whereas the absence of such correlations would falsify the proposed framework (Kiousis, Popescu, & Mitrook 2007; McCombs, Llamas, Lopez-Escobar, & Rey, 1997).

RESULTS

Based on the data, the top three issues receiving the most combined attention across the Obama, MoveOn.org and Obama in 30 Seconds advertising agendas during the 2008 U.S. presidential election primaries were the Iraq war, followed by fixing government, and health care. Rounding out the top five issues were jobs and the economy. These issues were followed in rank order by taxes, the environment, education, and energy/fuel. Table 1 reports the combined salience of issues across the three agendas as well as the salience of the issues for each individual agenda.

TABLE 1
Issue Frequencies (and Ranks) in YouTube Advertising During the 2008
U.S. Presidential Election Primaries

	Obama ads (rank)	MoveOn.org ads (rank)	Obama in 30 seconds ads (rank)	Total (rank)
Economy	11 (6)	2 (7)	13 (3)	26 (5)
Iraq war	15 (4)	21 (1)	27 (1)	63 (1)
Energy/fuel	4 (8)	0	4 (9)	8 (9)
Health care	20 (2)	7 (4)	16 (2)	43 (3)
Jobs	16 (3)	8 (3)	6 (8)	30 (4)
Fix government	29 (1)	19 (2)	13 (3)	61 (2)
Education	4 (8)	6 (5)	10 (5)	19 (8)
Environment	5 (7)	6 (5)	8 (6)	21 (7)
Taxes	15 (4)	2 (7)	7 (7)	24 (6)

Turning to the specific agendas, the Iraq war was the issue that received the most attention on the MoveOn.org ad agenda, followed by fix government and jobs. While fixing government and jobs were also two of the top three issues on the Obama ad agenda, the Iraq war ranked as only the fourth most salient issue in the Obama ads. The top five most salient issues on the Obama agenda were fix government, health care, jobs, and a tie between taxes and the Iraq war. As was the case with MoveOn.org, the most salient issue on the Obama in 30 Seconds ad agenda was also the Iraq war. The issue receiving the next most attention in the ad submissions was health care. Rounding out the top five issues were fixing government, the economy, and education. The issues of taxes and the environment were in the middle on all three agendas, whereas the energy/fuel issue received the least attention.

The top five issues receiving the most attention in the pages of *The Nation* were the Iraq war, fixing government, the economy, health care, and education. Table 2 reports the salience of the issues in media coverage by story type (editorials, columns, and articles).

Shifting to the hypothesis testing, H1 predicted that the salience of issues in MoveOn.org ads would be positively associated with the salience of issues in Obama in 30 Seconds ads. The data provided support for this hypothesis ($r_s = .60$, $p < .05$).

Table 3 displays the correlations of issue salience among the media coverage and the Obama, MoveOn.org, and Obama in 30 Seconds ad agendas.

H2 stated that the salience of issues in Obama campaign ads would be positively associated with the salience of issues in Obama in 30 Seconds ads. The data did not support this hypothesis.

TABLE 2
Issue Frequencies (and Ranks) in *The Nation* Magazine During the 2008 U.S. Presidential Election Primaries

	Editorials (rank)	Columns (rank)	Articles (rank)	Total (rank)
Economy	43 (3)	18 (3)	44 (2)	105 (3)
Iraq war	60 (1)	36 (1)	60 (1)	156 (1)
Energy/fuel	24 (6)	7 (8)	24 (8)	55 (8)
Health care	28 (5)	13 (5)	42 (3)	83 (4)
Jobs	18 (9)	10 (7)	19 (9)	47 (9)
Fix government	56 (2)	17 (4)	36 (5)	109 (2)
Education	24 (6)	20 (2)	38 (4)	82 (5)
Environment	34 (4)	13 (5)	32 (6)	79 (6)
Taxes	24 (6)	7 (8)	30 (7)	61 (7)

TABLE 3
Correlations of Issue Salience Among Online Advertising Agendas and
Media Coverage

	Obama YouTube ads	MoveOn.org YouTube ads	Obama in 30 seconds ads	The Nation media coverage
Obama YouTube ads	1.00			
MoveOn.org YouTube ads	0.66**	1.00		
Obama in 30 Seconds ads	0.41	0.60**	1.00	
The Nation media coverage	0.31	0.51*	0.93***	1.00

$^*p < .10.$ $^{**}p < .05.$ $^{***}p < .01.$

H3, which predicted that the salience of issues in MoveOn.org ads would be positively associated with the salience of issues in Obama campaign ads, received support ($r_s = .66$, $p < .05$).

H4 predicted a positive association between the salience of issues in the ads and the salience of issues in media coverage by *The Nation*. This hypothesis received robust support for the relationship between the coverage and the Obama in 30 Seconds ads ($r_s = .93$, $p < .01$) and weak support for the relationship between the coerage and the MoveOrg.ads ($r_s = 0.51$, $p < 0.10$). The data did not support this hypothesis for the Obama campaign ads.

Overall, the first set of hypotheses, which predicted first-level intermedia agenda-setting effects among the three ad agendas and the media agenda, received modest support.

The coding for second-level affective attributes revealed that approximately half (71 of 143) of the issues mentioned in the Obama ads were neutral or positive in valence, whereas only about a quarter (21 of 79) of the issues mentioned in the MoveOn.org ads fit this tone. Overall, the issues identified in the MoveOn.org ads were presented in a negative context (58 of 79), whereas the tone of the Obama ads was more balanced. Table 4 displays the salience of affective attributes in the Obama and MoveOn.org ads during the election primaries in more detail.

When considering the second set of hypotheses, which tested for the presence of compelling arguments, H5 predicted that the salience of affective attributes in MoveOn.org ads would be positively associated with the salience of issues in Obama in 30 Seconds ads. The data did not support this hypothesis as neither of the relationships among the MoveOn.org negative ads and Obama in 30 Seconds ads, and the MoveOn.org positive ads and Obama in 30 Seconds ads, were significant. Table 5 displays the affective attribute and issue salience relationships among the ad agendas.

TABLE 4
Affective Attributes Frequencies (and Ranks) in YouTube Ads During the 2008
U.S. Presidential Election Primaries

	Obama ads (rank)	MoveOn.org ads (rank)	Total (rank)
Economy			
Positive	0	1 (2)	1 (7)
Neutral	6 (2)	1 (4)	7 (2)
Negative	5 (5)	0	5 (7)
Iraq war			
Positive	0	0	0
Neutral	2 (3)	5 (1)	7 (2)
Negative	12 (2)	17 (1)	29 (2)
Energy/Fuel			
Positive	0	0	0
Neutral	1 (5)	0	1 (8)
Negative	3 (6)	0	3 (8)
Health care			
Positive	11 (1)	1 (2)	12 (1)
Neutral	1 (5)	2 (2)	3 (4)
Negative	8 (4)	3 (6)	11 (4)
Jobs			
Positive	5 (3)	0	5 (4)
Neutral	1 (5)	1 (4)	2 (5)
Negative	10 (3)	7 (3)	17 (3)
Fix government			
Positive	7 (2)	2 (1)	9 (2)
Neutral	2 (3)	0	2 (5)
Negative	20 (1)	17 (1)	37 (1)
Education			
Positive	2 (5)	0	2 (6)
Neutral	0	2 (2)	2 (5)
Negative	2 (8)	4 (5)	6 (6)
Environment			
Positive	2 (5)	1 (2)	3 (5)
Neutral	0	0	0
Negative	3 (6)	5 (4)	8 (5)
Taxes			
Positive	6 (3)	1 (2)	7 (3)
Neutral	8 (1)	0	8 (1)
Negative	1 (9)	2 (7)	3 (8)

H6, which stated that the salience of affective attributes in Obama
campaign ads would be positively associated with the salience of issues in
Obama in 30 Seconds ads, received mixed support. The data did not support
this hypothesis for the Obama positive ads, but a relationship approaching

TABLE 5

Affective Attribute and Issue Salience Relationships Among Obama, MoveOn.org, and Obama in 30 Seconds Ads

	Positive MoveOn.org YouTube ads	Negative MoveOn.org YouTube ads	Positive Obama YouTube ads	Negative Obama YouTube ads	MoveOn.org YouTube ads	Obama YouTube ads	Obama in 30 seconds ads
Positive MoveOn.org YouTube ads	1.00						
Negative MoveOn.org YouTube ads	0.24	1.00					
Positive Obama YouTube ads	0.76***	0.25	1.00				
Negative Obama YouTube ads	0.11	0.67**	0.13	1.00			
MoveOn.org YouTube ads	0.19	0.94***	0.31	0.80**	1.00		
Obama YouTube ads	0.56*	0.52*	0.72**	0.70**	0.66**	1.00	
Obama in 30 Seconds ads	0.17	0.42	0.09	0.51*	0.60**	0.41	1.00

*$p < .10$. **$p < .05$. ***$p < .01$.

significance was found for the Obama negative ads ($r_s = .51$, $p < .10$). This second-level relationship between the Obama negative ads and the Obama in 30 Seconds issue ads was higher than the first-level relationship between the two issue agendas, thereby demonstrating the subtleties among agendas that may be detected by testing for the compelling-arguments hypothesis.

H7 predicted that the salience of affective attributes in Obama campaign ads would be positively associated with the salience of issues in MoveOn.org ads. The data provided mixed support for this hypothesis. The data did not support this hypothesis for the Obama positive ads, but a robust relationship was found among the Obama negative ads and the MoveOn.org ads ($r_s = .80$, $p < .01$). This second-level relationship between the Obama negative attribute agenda and the MoveOn.org issue agenda exceeds the first-level relationship between the two issue agendas ($r_s = .66$, $p < .05$).

Finally, RQ1 asked whether the MoveOn.org ads, Obama campaign ads, or progressive media coverage would be the most strongly associated with the Obama in 30 Seconds ads regarding the salience of issues. Based on the results of the zero-order correlations, the media coverage was the most strongly associated ($r_s = .93$, $p < .01$) with the citizen-activist created Obama in 30 Seconds ads. To more rigorously assess RQ1, second-order partial correlations were also computed to control for the effect of the other two agendas on the bivariate relationship of interest. These partial correlations revealed that the strongest linkage ($r = .91$, $p < .01$) remained between the media coverage and the citizen activist-created ads. This robust linkage, after controlling for the MoveOn.org and Obama ads, confirms the original media and public agenda-setting hypothesis (McCombs & Shaw, 1972).

DISCUSSION

This study analyzed first and second-level intermedia agenda-setting relationships in the underexplored context of political activist online advertising and explicitly partisan media coverage during a presidential primary. Specifically, this study tested for the transfer of issue and affective attribute salience among political media content appearing in *The Nation*, a progressive news media outlet, and YouTube ads created by the campaign of Democratic candidate Barack Obama, Web-based progressive activist group MoveOn.org, and citizen activists that took part in the Obama in 30 Seconds contest during the 2008 U.S. presidential election primaries. MoveOn.org, which officially endorsed Obama for president during the primaries, held an online contest in the spring of 2008 called Obama in

30 Seconds in which it encouraged citizen activists to make positive ads about the candidate (Zeleny & Healy, 2008).

First-Level Agenda-Setting Effects

The data provide modest evidence of first-level intermedia agenda-setting effects. Significant positive relationships were found among the issue agendas of the *The Nation* and the Obama in 30 Seconds ads, the MoveOn.org ads and the Obama in 30 Seconds ads, and the MoveOn.org ads and the Obama campaign ads. Of interest, the strongest first-level correlation ($r_s = .93$, $p < .01$) was among the partisan media coverage and the Obama in 30 Seconds ads, suggesting that the political issue priorities of *The Nation* and these citizen activists, at least at this phase of the campaign, were highly similar. Although this study's focus on exploring intermedia agenda-setting effects among sets of political ads and coverage that all support the *same candidate* is unique, these findings fit with previous agenda-setting studies involving political ads, which have generally found evidence of first-level effects (Ghorpade, 1986; Golan et al., 2007; Lopez-Escobar et al., 1998; Roberts & McCombs, 1994).

Continuing with a discussion of the first-level findings, the association between the MoveOn.org ads and citizen activist-created Obama in 30 Seconds ads was significant, whereas the association between the Obama campaign ads and Obama in 30 Seconds ads was not. This finding intuitively makes sense as many of the ad submissions were likely made by individuals who are also MoveOn.org members. Therefore, their political issue agendas may have already been shaped by exposure to previous MoveOn.org-controlled communications efforts, whereas the Obama agenda may have been less well known at this point in the campaign cycle. Conversely, this stronger relationship could also be due to claims by MoveOn.org that it polls its members to learn the most salient issues on their minds and then it adapts its agenda to emphasize these issues (Solomon, 2005). In any case, given the seemingly growing influence of social media-enabled grass roots activism on the modern campaign, a deeper understanding of the relationship between the agendas of activist groups and citizen activists would appear to be an area ripe for further inquiry. The agenda-melding literature (e.g., Ragas & Roberts, 2009; Shaw, Hamm, & Knott, 2000; Shaw, Hamm, & Terry, 2006; Shaw, McCombs, Weaver, & Hamm, 1999; Shaw, Stevenson, & Hamm, 2001) could be a natural path for this exploration. Agenda-melding posits that groups represent a "collected agenda of issues" and "one joins a group by adopting an agenda," thereby "melding" their individual agenda with the group agenda (Shaw et al., 1999, p. 12).

Second-Level Agenda-Setting Effects

Regarding second-level intermedia agenda effects, the evidence was more mixed. The second set of hypotheses specifically tested for the affective aspect of the compelling-arguments hypothesis, which asserts that when a particular attribute of an object is emphasized on one agenda, there may be a shift in the overall salience afforded that object on another agenda (Ghanem, 1997). Weak evidence for a compelling arguments relationship was found between the Obama negative ads and the Obama in 30 Seconds ads ($r_s = .51$, $p < .10$). Stronger evidence for compelling arguments was found between the Obama negative ads and the MoveOn.org ads ($r_s = .80$, $p < .01$). From a theory-building perspective, at least two previous studies (Golan et al., 2007; Sheafer, 2007) that have specifically analyzed the affective aspect of the compelling argument hypothesis also found evidence for this hypothesis among attribute agendas that are *negative* in tone. The salience of negative attributes could be explained in part by research which has shown that individuals pay more attention to negative information than positive information (Cacioppo & Berntson, 1994; Jordan, 1965; Lau, 1982, 1985).

The strong relationship between the Obama negative ads and the overall MoveOn.org ads also raises interesting questions about the direction of influence among these agendas. Were MoveOn.org's ads influenced by the issues emphasized in Obama's negative ads or did the Obama campaign consciously decide to run positive issue ads that appealed more to the general public, while running negative ads that spoke more to the issues of its activist group supporters like MoveOn.org? Identifying and analyzing these subtle relationships would be impossible without probing for two-levels of agenda-setting effects, thereby underscoring the value in probing for the interplay between issue and attribute agendas. As noted by Golan et al. (2007), "attribute salience measures are not only important for understanding the formation of attribute agendas but object agendas as well" (p. 438).

Theoretical Contributions

Overall, this study makes several noteworthy theoretical contributions. First, this study successfully builds on the small body of previous agenda-setting research focused on political ads while tying this literature to the broader scholarship on intermedia agenda-setting and the compelling-arguments hypothesis. Second, although a group of studies has previously discussed the agenda-setting role of *social activist groups* (Carpenter, 2007; Hicks, 2004; Holzer, 2007; Kim, 2006; Pralle, 2006a,b; Schiffer, 2006), this study represents one of the first investigations to closely analyze the communication efforts of a Web-based *political activist group* during the early stages of an election contest and how these efforts relate to the agendas of citizen activists and a candidate's campaign. In addition, this is one of the first agenda-setting studies to gauge a subset of public opinion, in this case the political issue priorities of citizen activists, by analyzing consumer-generated content on the Web. Finally, this is also one of the first investigations to test for agenda-setting relationships using an explicitly partisan media outlet. Most prior agenda-setting research has focused on mainstream nonpartisan media outlets, which attempt to provide unbiased and balanced coverage of the candidates and political issues.

Limitations and Future Research

In terms of limitations, this study breaks new ground in establishing the presence of intermedia agenda-setting relationships among a political activist group, citizen activists, and a candidate's campaign, but the direction of influence cannot be determined by the present investigation. Therefore, future research in this area should consider using a longitudinal design to begin determining *causal relationships*. Further, the findings in the current study are based on the use of one type of information subsidy (online ads on YouTube channels), one partisan media source (*The Nation*), in one type of election contest (a U.S. presidential election), at one period (the primary phase before the general election period), and with one political activist group (MoveOn.org). Replications are needed before more definitive conclusions may be drawn. Future intermedia research involving political activist groups should consider analyzing other classic information subsidies, such as news releases, as well as emerging information subsidies, such as blogs, SMS text messages, and other online social-interactive media. Future research could also compare the candidate, political activist group, and citizen activist agendas with the mainstream news media (nonpartisan media outlets as opposed to explicitly partisan sources) and public agendas, to begin building out a broader picture of these relationships.

The "fourth stage" of agenda-setting research (McCombs, 1992) has traditionally attempted to answer the question of who sets the media agenda. Although political activist groups such as MoveOn.org seemingly attempt to influence the media agenda (Babbin, 2007), there are also signs that they attempt to influence the agenda of the political party and candidates that they support (Herszenhorn, 2007). With this in mind, a question worth exploring more fully in the future may be, Who sets the candidate agenda? Previous agenda-setting scholarship indicates that political candidates, as well as elected officials, not only attempt to set the media agenda but also react to media coverage, thus at times forming a reciprocal relationship

(Kiousis, Mitrook, Popescu, Shields, & Seltzer, 2006; Lopez-Escobar et al., 1998; Sweetser et al., 2008). Recent research on the new concept of intercandidate agenda-setting (Kiousis & Shields, 2008; Tedesco, 2005), which posits that competing political campaigns may impact the agendas of one another, also gets at the question of *who sets the candidate agenda*. A bidirectional relationship may well exist between political advocacy, activist, and special interest groups with the candidates they support, or there may be instances where the candidate clearly leads the agenda-setting dance and vice versa. In short, the study of the interplay among political activist, political candidate-controlled communication efforts, and partisan news media coverage adds an exciting new dimension to the agenda-setting tradition and political communication research as a whole.

REFERENCES

Amazon.com. (2009). Product description. *The Nation*. Retrieved from http://www.amazon.com/The-Nation/dp/B000CNEFRE

Andrews, K. T., & Edwards, B. (2004). Advocacy organizations in the U.S. political process. *Annual Review of Sociology, 30*(1), 479–506.

Atkin, C., & Heald, G. (1976). Effects of political advertising. *Public Opinion Quarterly, 40*, 216–228.

Babbin, J. (2007, October). MoveOn.org reshaped the media battlefield. *Human Events, 63*(33), 7.

Bowers, T. A. (1973). Newspaper political advertising and the agenda-setting function. *Journalism Quarterly, 50*, 552–556.

Boyle, T. P. (2001). Intermedia agenda setting in the 1996 presidential election. *Journalism & Mass Communication Quarterly, 78*(1), 26–44.

Cacioppo, J. T., & Berntson, G. G. (1994). Relationships between attitudes and evaluative space: A critical-review, with emphasis on the separability of positive and negative substrates. *Psychological Bulletin, 115*, 401–423.

Carpenter, R. C. (2007). Setting the advocacy agenda: Theorizing issue emergence and nonemergence in transnational advocacy networks. *International Studies Quarterly, 51*(1), 99–120.

Cohen, B. (1963). *The press and foreign policy*. Princeton, NJ: Princeton University Press.

Coleman, R., & Banning, S. (2006). Network TV news' affective framing of the presidential candidates: Evidence for a second-level agenda-setting effect through visual framing. *Journalism & Mass Communication Quarterly, 83*, 313–328.

Coleman, R., & McCombs, M. (2007). The young and agenda-less? Exploring age-related differences in agenda setting on the youngest generation, baby boomers, and the civic generation. *Journalism & Mass Communication Quarterly, 84*, 495–508.

deJong, W., Shaw, M., & Stammers, N. (Eds.). (2005). *Global activism global media*. London: Pluto Press.

Ghanem, S. (1997). Filling in the tapestry: The second level of agenda setting. In M. McCombs, D. L. Shaw & D. Weaver (Eds.), *Communication and democracy: Exploring the intellectual frontiers in agenda-setting theory* (pp. 3–14). Mahwah, NJ: Erlbaum.

Ghorpade, S. (1986). Agenda setting: A test of advertising's neglected function. *Journal of Advertising Research, 26*(4), 23–27.

Golan, G. J., Kiousis, S. K., & McDaniel, M. L. (2007). Second-level agenda setting and polit-ical advertising. *Journalism Studies*, *8*, 432–443.

Hayes, C. (2008). MoveOn at ten. *The Nation*. Retrieved August 6, 2008, from http://www.thenation.com/doc/20080804/hayes

Herszenhorn, D. (2007, September 21). Senate approves resolution denouncing MoveOn.org ad. *New York Times*, p. A16.

Hicks, B. (2004). Setting agenda and shaping activism: EU influence on Central and Eastern European environmental movements. *Environmental Politics*, *13*(1), 216–233.

Holsti, O. (1969). *Content analysis for the social sciences & humanities.* Reading, MA: Addison-Wesley.

Holzer, B. (2007). Framing the corporation: Royal Dutch/Shell and human rights woes in Nigeria. *Journal of Consumer Policy*, *30*, 281–301.

Jordan, N. (1965). The asymmetry of liking and disliking: A phenomenon meriting further reflection and research. *Public Opinion Quarterly*, *29*, 315–322.

Kim, A. E. (2006). Civic activism and Korean democracy: The impact of blacklisting campaigns in the 2000 and 2004 general elections. *The Pacific Review*, *19*, 519–542.

Kiousis, S. (2005). Compelling arguments and attitude strength: Exploring the impact of second-level agenda setting on public opinion of presidential candidate images. *The Harvard Journal of Press/Politics*, *10*(3), 3–27.

Kiousis, S., Mitrook, M., Popescu, C., Shields, A., & Seltzer, T. (2006, June). *First- and second-level agenda building and agenda setting: Terrorism, the president and the media.* Paper presented at the annual meeting of the International Communication Association, Dresden, Germany.

Kiousis, S., Mitrook, M., Wu, X., & Seltzer, T. (2006). First- and second-level agenda-building and agenda-setting effects: Exploring the linkages among candidate news releases, media coverage, and public opinion during the 2002 Florida gubernatorial election. *Journal of Public Relations Research*, *18*, 265–285.

Kiousis, S., Popescu, C., & Mitrook, M. (2007). Understanding influence on corporate reputation: An examination of public relations efforts, media coverage, public opinion, and financial performance from an agenda-building and agenda-setting perspective. *Journal of Public Relations Research*, *19*(2), 147–165.

Kiousis, S., & Shields, A. (2008). Intercandidate agenda-setting in presidential elections: Issue and attribute agendas in the 2004 campaign. *Public Relations Review*, *34*, 325–330.

Lau, R. R. (1982). Negativity in political perception. *Political Behavior*, *4*, 353–377.

Lau, R. R. (1985). Two explanations for negativity effects in political-behavior. *American Journal of Political Science*, *29*, 199–138.

Lopez-Escobar, E., Llamas, J. P., McCombs, M., & Lennon, F. R. (1998). Two levels of agenda setting among advertising and news in the 1995 Spanish elections. *Political Communication*, *15*, 225–238.

McCaughey, M., & Ayers, M. D. (Eds.). (2003). *Cyberactivism: Online activism in theory and practice.* New York: Routledge.

McCombs, M. (1992). Explorers and surveyors: Expanding strategies for agenda-setting research. *Journalism Quarterly*, *69*, 813–824.

McCombs, M. (2005). A look at agenda-setting: Past, present and future. *Journalism Studies*, *6*, 543–557.

McCombs, M. (2006). *Setting the agenda: The mass media and public opinion.* Malden, MA: Polity Press.

McCombs, M. E., & Bell, T. (1996). The agenda-setting role of mass communication. In M. Salwen & D. Stacks (Eds.), *An integrated approach to communication theory and research* (pp. 93–110). Mahwah, NJ: Erlbaum.

McCombs, M., & Evatt, D. (1995). Los temas y los aspectos: Explorando una nueva dimension de la agenda setting. [Objects and attributes: Exploring a new dimension of agenda setting]. *Comunicacion y Socieded, 8*(1), 7–32.

McCombs, M., & Ghanem, S. I. (2003). The convergence of agenda setting and framing. In S. D. Reese, O. H. Gandy & A. E. Grant (Eds.), *Framing public life: Perspectives on media and our understanding of the social world* (pp. 67–81). Mahwah, NJ: Erlbaum.

McCombs, M., Llamas, J. P., Lopez-Escobar, E., & Rey, F. (1997). Candidate images in Spanish elections: Second-level agenda-setting effects. *Journalism & Mass Communication Quarterly, 74*, 703–717.

McCombs, M. E., Lopez-Escobar, E., & Llamas, J. P. (2000). Setting the agenda of attributes in the 1996 Spanish General Election. *Journal of Communication, 50*, 77–92.

McCombs, M. E., & Shaw, D. L. (1972). The agenda-setting function of mass media. *Public Opinion Quarterly 36*, 176–187.

McCombs, M. E., & Shaw, D. L. (1993). The evolution of agenda-setting research: Twenty-five years in the marketplace of ideas. *Journal of Communication, 43*(2), 58–68.

Miller, M. M., Andsager, J. L., & Reichert, B. P. (1998). Framing the presidents in presidential primaries: issues and images in press releases and news coverage. *Journalism & Mass Communication Quarterly, 75*, 312–324.

Pew Internet and American Life Project. (2007, January 17). *Election 2006 online.* Retrieved May 2, 2010, from http://www.pewinternet.org/Reports/2007/Election-2006-Online.aspx

Pralle, S. (2006a). The "mouse that roared": Agenda setting in Canadian pesticides politics. *The Policy Studies Journal, 34*, 171–194.

Pralle, S. B. (2006b). Timing and sequence in agenda-setting and policy change: A comparative study of lawn care pesticide politics in Canada and the US. *Journal of European Public Policy, 13*, 987–1005.

Price, T. (2004, September). Cyberpolitics: Do computers and the Internet enhance democracy? *CQ Researcher, 14*, 757–780.

Ragas, M. W., & Roberts, M. S. (2009). Agenda-setting and agenda-melding in an age of horizontal and vertical media: A new theoretical lens for virtual brand communities. *Journalism & Mass Communication Quarterly, 86*(1), 45–64.

Roberts, M., & McCombs, M. (1994). Agenda setting and political advertising: Origins of the news agenda. *Political Communication, 11*, 249–262.

Schiffer, A. J. (2006). Blogswarms and press norms: News coverage of the Downing Street memo controversy. *Journalism & Mass Communication Quarterly, 83*, 494–510.

Schoenbach, K., & Semetko, H. A. (1992). Agenda-setting, agenda-reinforcing or agenda-deflating? A study of the 1990 German national election. *Journalism Quarterly, 69*, 837–846.

Scott, W. A. (1955). Reliability of content analysis. The case of nominal scale coding. *Public Opinion Quarterly, 19*, 321–325.

Shaw, D. L., Hamm, B. J., & Knott, D. L. (2000). Technological change, agenda challenge and social melding: Mass media studies and the four ages of place, class, mass and space. *Journalism Studies, 1*(1), 57–79.

Shaw, D. L., Hamm, B. J., & Terry, T. C. (2006). Vertical versus horizontal media. *Military Review, 86*, 13–25.

Shaw, D. L., McCombs, M., Weaver, D. H., & Hamm, B. J. (1999). Individuals, groups, and agenda melding: A theory of social dissonance. *International Journal of Public Opinion Research, 11*(1), 2–24.

Shaw, D. L., Stevenson, R. L., & Hamm, B. J. (2001). *Agenda setting theory and public opinion studies in a post-mass media age.* Paper presented at the annual meeting of the World Association for Public Opinion Research, Rome, Italy.

Sheafer, T. (2007). How to evaluate it: The role of story-evaluative tone in agenda setting and priming. *Journal of Communication, 57*(1), 21–39.

Solomon, N. (2005, May). Iraq withdrawal and MoveOn.org. *Humanist, 65*(3), 7–10.

Sutherland, M., & Galloway, J. (1981). Role of advertising: Persuasion or agenda setting? *Journal of Advertising Research, 21*(5), 25–29.

Sweetser, K. D., Golan, G. J., & Wanta, W. (2008). Intermedia agenda setting in television, advertising, and blogs during the 2004 election. *Mass Communication and Society, 11*, 197–216.

Tedesco, J. C. (2001). Issue and strategy agenda-setting in the 2000 presidential primaries. *American Behavioral Scientist, 44*, 2048–2067.

Tedesco, J. C. (2005). Issue and strategy agenda setting in the 2004 presidential election: Exploring the candidate–journalist relationship. *Journalism Studies, 6*, 187–201.

Weaver, D. H. (2007). Thoughts on agenda setting, framing, and priming. *Journal of Communication, 57*(1), 142–147.

Yioutas, J., & Segvic, I. (2003). Revisiting the Clinton/Lewinsky scandal: The convergence of agenda setting and framing. *Journalism & Mass Communication Quarterly, 80*, 567–582.

Zeleny, J., & Healy, P. (2008, February 2). Obama wins endorsement of MoveOn.org. *New York Times.*

The 2008 Presidential Campaign: Political Cynicism in the Age of Facebook, MySpace, and YouTube

Gary Hanson
School of Journalism & Mass Communication
Kent State University

Paul Michael Haridakis, Audrey Wagstaff Cunningham, Rekha Sharma, and J. D. Ponder
School of Communication Studies
Kent State University

Considerable research over the years has been devoted to ascertaining the impact of media use on political cynicism. The impact of the Internet has been difficult to assess because it is not a single monolithic medium. For example, the 2008 presidential campaign was the first presidential campaign in which popular social networking sites such as Facebook, MySpace, and YouTube were widely available to voters. Therefore, the campaign offered the first opportunity to explore the influence of these social media on political cynicism. In this study, we examined whether the use of such social media influenced political cynicism. We also considered the influence of user background characteristics (e.g., self-efficacy, locus of control, political orientation, demographics, and influence of family and friends), motives for using social media for political information, and users' elaboration on political content. Several individual differences were stronger predictors of political cynicism than was social media use. In fact, social networking use was a negative predictor of political cynicism. Results supported uses and gratifications' notions that the influence of social media on political cynicism is more attributable to user background and media-use differences than to sheer use of these popular sites.

The 2008 presidential campaign was the first to play out in the world of YouTube, Facebook, MySpace, and political blogging—the major Internet-based social media. These social media provide a new form of mediated communication that gives the audience access to on-demand content and the ability to share and discuss it with others (e.g., Levy, 2008; Papacharissi, 2009; Spigel, 2009). The most popular social networking sites (SNS) are relative newcomers: MySpace went online in 2003, Facebook in 2004, and YouTube in 2005. In the 2008 presidential campaign, social networks provided a new form of political communication for citizens to use to learn about candidates and issues (Dobbin, 2007; Makinen & Kuira, 2008). Television stations and newspapers used these new media portals to engage viewers and readers (Armbruster, 2008; Atkin, 2008; Whitney, 2008). Traditional media companies embraced social media at a time when the companies themselves faced significant economic challenges (*The State of the News Media 2007*, 2008). Media companies were not alone. The campaigns themselves, particularly the Obama campaign, used social networking and interactive media to reach its voters (Carr & Stelter, 2008; Cohen, 2008; Learmonth, 2008). More importantly, these social media provided an opportunity for ordinary citizens to create their own political content, distribute it online, and comment on the content created by others. Each of these social media is distinct. For example, YouTube is primarily a video-sharing site that permits users to both view and upload video content and commentary. On the other hand, sites such as Facebook are more textual and are designed more for direct interpersonal and social connection. But an important similarity among these social media and a defining attribute of each is the fact that they are more user centered than their traditional media counterparts; therefore, they allow forms of political interaction that weren't available in previous presidential campaigns.

The 2008 campaign also played out against a long-standing tradition of voter cynicism. Much has been written about the influence of older, more traditional media (e.g., newspapers, radio, television) on increased voter cynicism (Cappella & Jamieson, 1997; J. W. Koch, 2003; Miller, 1974; Pinkleton, Um, & Austin, 2002). The Internet has become an additional source of political information with its own potential to influence voter attitudes.

However, the impact of social media on political cynicism has been difficult to assess because early studies tended to treat the Internet as a single entity. Few studies examined the use of individual categories of Web sites (e.g., news sites or opinion sites), and fewer still examined those specific sites that allow for social interaction (e.g., Ancu & Cozma, 2009; Sweetser & Lariscy, 2008). The 2008 campaign was the first opportunity for researchers to study this phenomenon in a national presidential election. This inquiry is important, because social media introduced a new set of vectors along which information and opinion can travel—often directly from user to user. As a result, users are now in control of more of the distribution path. The ability for users to exercise greater control over their political media choices makes it appropriate to apply a user-centered media effects perspective to assess the effect of media use, in this case, the degree to which it predicts levels of voter cynicism.

Uses and gratifications has been the most widely used audience-centered perspective guiding media research in the last 35 years. Uses and gratifications is a media-effects perspective that emphasizes the role of the individual in the media use and effects process. As such, it focuses not just on media influence but also on how use and effects are influenced by users' motives and background characteristics. Guided by this theoretical perspective, the goals of this study are twofold: to examine the relationship between three types of social media use and levels of political cynicism and to examine the relative contribution of users' background characteristics, motives for using social media for political information, and the use of social media to explain political cynicism.

LITERATURE REVIEW

Political Information

Political and communication scholars have long asserted that accurate information is necessary for informed and rational voting decisions (Benoit & Hansen, 2004; Berelson, 1966). Lazarsfeld, Berelson, and Gaudet (1944) identified three primary functions of political information: activation, reinforcement, and conversion—a pattern consistent in subsequent research

(Finkel, 1993; Ohr & Schrott, 2001). Television has been the predominant source of public affairs information since the mid-1960s (Bouza, 2004; Gilliam & Iyengar, 2000; Landreville, 2007; Ostroff & Sandell, 1984). Beginning in the late 1990s, the Internet gained in popularity as a source for political news, particularly for college students (Lee, 2006). The advantages of the Internet for political information have been well documented (Kaid, 2002; Kaye & Johnson, 2002; Robbin & Buente, 2008). Bimber (1998) argued that the Internet could facilitate greater political participation by giving voters the ability to learn about government, discuss issues and contact their representatives, and register to vote. Internet users who use the medium for information exchange show a higher percentage of interpersonal trust and civic engagement (Shah, Kwak, & Holbert, 2001). Althaus and Tewksbury (2000) reported that young respondents used the Web for political surveillance as a supplement to more traditional media content.

Of course, in addition to media, citizens receive political information from interpersonal sources as well (Campus, Pasquino, & Vaccari, 2008; Jackson-Beeck, 1979; Kingdon, 1970; N. S. Koch, 1994). The intersection between political information from the media and political information from interpersonal networks is an important point for this study. SNS on the Internet provide some of the same functions as interpersonal communication: user communities (Doddington & Adams, 2007), friendship maintenance (Gennaro & Dutton, 2007), social interaction (Ho & Niederdeppe, 2008), and the development of personal identities and relationships online (Jones, Millermaier, Goya-Martinez, & Schuler, 2008).

Social Networks and Politics

Early research pertaining to the relationship between membership in social networks and political involvement suggested that the membership stimulates a collective interest in politics (Putnam, 2000), makes people available to elites for mobilization (Leighley, 1996), and helps people learn skills that make participation easier (Brady, Verba, & Schlozman, 1995). More recently, scholars have found that social networks are a rapid way to disseminate innovative information and values (Gibson, 2001).

Online SNS are a relatively new phenomenon in politics. Potential voters can use online sources such as Facebook, MySpace, LinkedIn, and even YouTube to interact with and obtain information from others. They can form various groups that support particular candidates or issues, seek out political information, engage in online discussions with others about issues or candidates, blog about political issues, and even share videos (Boyd, 2008; Brown, Broderick, & Lee, 2007; Lange, 2007; Price, Nir, & Cappella, 2006; Xenos & Foot, 2007).

Brown et al. (2007) found that individuals who participate in online social environments such as SNS are likely to experience a sense of understanding, connection, involvement, and interaction with others who participate in these environments.

This representative research suggests that newer forms of social media may offer a unique avenue for political communication that may affect political cynicism much differently than political communication in presocial networking media eras.

Cynicism

Researchers have documented a loss of confidence in American institutions for nearly half a century, specifically the public's dissatisfaction with the political process (Lipset & Schneider, 1983, 1987; Miller, 1974). Cynicism has been defined as a distrust of the political system (Dennis & Webster, 1975). Scholars draw the distinction between cynicism (considered to be unhealthy) and a healthy skepticism of government and suggest that the media cultivate the former (Cappella & Jamieson, 1997).

The media's relationship to political cynicism has been well documented (Cappella & Jamieson, 1997; de Vreese, 2005; de Vreese & Elenbaas, 2008; Pinkleton, Austin, & Fortman, 1998). As one might expect, much of the research has focused on television (Kaid, 2002; Leshner & McKean, 1997; Robinson, 1976), particularly on the effects of news and negative political advertising (de Vreese, 2005; de Vreese & Elenbaas, 2008; Forrest & Weseley, 2007; Jasperson & Hyun Jung, 2007; Kaid, 2002; Kaid, Postelnicu, Landreville, Hyun Jung, & LeGrange, 2007; Newton, 1999; Palser, 2007; Schenck-Hamlin & Procter, 2000). Much of this research indicates that consumption of media messages lead to cynicism, but the findings are not always consistent. For example, Pinkleton, Austin, and Fortman (1998) and Austin and Pinkleton (1999) found that active media use was a negative predictor of cynicism.

Researchers also have discovered that the media platforms make a difference. Kaid (2002) found that campaign ads on television and the Internet reported cynicism differently. Lee (2006) found that the perceived quality of political Web sites might predict cynicism. Hwang, Shah, and Cho (2008) found that media distrust was positively related to citizens' online information seeking. Sweetser and Kaid (2008) found that levels of cynicism varied according to exposure to political statements on blogs.

The 2008 campaign provides the first presidential campaign to assess the impact of these new forms of social media on the political process—germane to this study, their role in enhancing or reducing political cynicism. These newer media clearly put more control in the hands of users, who can tailor their interaction with media content to meet their specific needs. This attribute makes the application of a user-centered media perspective particularly amenable to studying such media use (Hanson & Haridakis, 2008; Ruggiero, 2000).

Uses and Gratifications

Uses and gratifications has been one of the most influential audience-centered perspectives applied to study media use and effects for more than 35 years. Uses and gratifications emphasizes the individual in the individual-media use-effects relationship. As such, the emphasis is on what people do with the media rather than on what the media do to them (Klapper, 1963). It assumes that people use media purposively, selectively and actively to satisfy their needs and wants.

Uses and gratifications suggests that media effects are the result of a confluence of factors working in concert. In addition to audience members' social and psychological background characteristics, uses and gratifications focuses on the role of motives for selecting and using media, and the selection of specific media and their content. Researchers guided by this theoretical perspective try to account for these numerous factors to explain how and why people use various mediated and interpersonal channels to satisfy their needs and desires. In sum, a contemporary uses and gratifications model suggests that the route to media effects depends on one's background characteristics, which influence motives for selecting and using media. Motives, in turn, influence how actively media are used. Together, these variables influence consequences of that use. Although uses and gratifications suggests that people use media purposively for need satisfaction, it recognizes that many effects, if not most, are unintended (Katz, Blumler, & Gurevitch, 1974).

Uses and gratifications has been applied to study the use of media for political information (Chaffee & Kanihan, 1997), motives for doing so (Kaye & Johnson, 2002, 2004; McLeod & Becker, 1974), and political media-use effects (Eveland, 2004). Ancu and Cozma (2009) applied a uses and gratifications model to a study of SNS in the 2008 campaign and found that users were motivated primarily by the desire for social interaction.

The on-demand nature of social media and the different types of social media available (e.g., video sharing sites, SNS) provide users with the opportunity to make a wide range of mediated communication choices—from traditional and nontraditional media fare (e.g., news stories, campaign videos, and amateur video mash-ups) to interpersonal and social uses (e.g., Facebook pages, posting comments and opinions, forwarding interesting Web links).

According to the uses and gratifications model guiding this study, then, the route to effects begins with consideration of important background characteristics. In the context of political media use, the literature suggests that several variables are potentially salient. These include self-efficacy, locus of control, political orientation, and the influence of one's family and friends.

Background Characteristics

Political self-efficacy. Campbell, Gurin, and Miller (1954) defined political efficacy as "the feeling that individual political action does have, or can have an impact upon the political process" (p. 187). Tedesco (2006) suggested that political efficacy is significantly greater among young interactive Web users than young noninteractive ones. There is evidence that higher levels of political self-efficacy are related to lower levels of political cynicism (Pinkleton & Austin, 2002, 2004).

Locus of control. Locus of control is a personality trait that distinguishes between internally controlled individuals (i.e., individuals who believe they control events in their lives) and externally controlled individuals (i.e., individuals who believe that events in a person's life are controlled by forces other than themselves; Rotter, 1966). In the context of media use, locus of control has been used to predict viewer motives and perceptions (Haridakis, 2002). The present study included locus of control because it is logical that people who felt they exerted greater control would be less cynical about their ability to influence the political system as it relates to them.

Political orientation. Research suggests that political orientation influences political media use and effects. Some research has suggested that political conservatives are change resistant, dogmatic, and satisfied with societal inequalities (Jost, Glaser, & Kruglanski, 2003). Other research has suggested that during the 2004 election, disenfranchised liberals turned to Weblogs to share information and to vent (Kaye & Johnson, 2006).

Influence of family and friends on political behavior. Researchers have recognized political socialization as a complex phenomenon involving numerous information-gathering strategies and communication channels resulting in myriad attitudinal and behavioral outcomes. Along with media use, scholars have considered the importance of interpersonal communication in the formation and articulation of political opinions as well as other kinds of participation (Kim, Wyatt, & Katz, 1999; McLeod, Scheufele, & Moy, 1999; Moy & Gastil, 2006; Scheufele, 2002). In a study of young minority voters, interpersonal communication ranked most frequently as a source of political information, followed by Internet and TV news (Jasperson & Hyun Jung, 2007). In addition, young voters who watched national television news, read the newspaper, listened to political talk radio, watched C-SPAN regularly, and engaged in interpersonal conversations about politics reported lower levels of cynicism.

Motives.   The study of motivation for using media has been a central focus of uses and gratifications research. The needs and desires people seek to satisfy are viewed as being reflected in their motives for using media and other communication channels. Over the years, researchers have explored people's possible motives for attending to political fare (McLeod & Becker, 1974) and for using specific media such as the Internet for political fare (Johnson & Kaye, 2003; Kaye & Johnson, 2002). These include seeking information, entertainment, relaxation, social utility, and guidance. In addition, when it comes to using the Internet or specific Internet functions such as YouTube, some users are motivated, in part, because of the convenience of online use (Hanson & Haridakis, 2008; Papacharissi & Rubin, 2000).

Elaboration.   Motivation is linked to audience activity. It is important to recognize that some people are more interested in politics and therefore are more active and involved when seeking political information about the campaign. Perse (1990) suggested that one way people exhibit that involvement is with their level of elaboration (i.e., thinking about the content and what it means). Eveland (2004) discovered that anticipation of future dialogue (which may be the case with those who use SNS) motivates individuals to think about politics.

Research Questions

Researchers should consider the impact of each new medium on the political process. As noted earlier, much as been written about the effect of media content on voter cynicism, but the results aren't conclusive. Some studies suggest that media use is a positive predictor of cynicism, whereas other studies (e.g., Pinkleton & Austin, 2001, 2002) question the impact of sheer media use or exposure on political cynicism. Given this lack of agreement on the influence of older media on political cynicism, it is prudent to examine the impact of newer social media on political cynicism with a series of research questions that may help clear up the ambiguity. The first research question looks at the three forms of social media examined in the study: SNS, such as Facebook; video sharing sites, such as YouTube; and the general category of political blogs.

> RQ1a: How does use of social networking Web sites relate to users' self-reported levels of political cynicism?

RQ1b: How does use of video sharing Web sites relate to users' self-reported levels of political cynicism?

RQ1c: How does use of political blogging Web sites relate to users' self-reported levels of political cynicism?

According to the tenets of uses and gratifications referenced earlier, media effects are due to much more than sheer exposure. Effects are the consequence of various factors working together. Uses and gratifications suggests that (a) individual background characteristics of media users (b) influence motives for using media for campaign-related content, which in turn (c) influence social media selection and amount of media consumed, (d) elaboration on the content, and ultimately the outcome of interest: (e) cynicism. The principal research question of the study asked about the relative contribution of each of these antecedent variables in predicting political cynicism.

RQ2: How do user background characteristics, motives, types and amount of social media use and elaboration on political content obtained predict political cynicism.

METHODS

Sample

Students in a large lecture course at a midwestern university were asked to complete survey forms for the study. The course is a liberal studies course that draws students from all majors across the university. In addition, the students recruited other participants based on a quota sample that reflected the statistical abstract of the age breakdown of voters in the state in which the research was conducted. All participants included in the study completed a 168-question printed questionnaire during the week before the 2008 general election.

A total of 467 questionnaires (242 from the class sample and 225 from the quota sample) provided usable data. The sample was 65.7% women (coded 1) and 34.3% men (coded 0). The age range was 18 to 93 ($M = 30.19$, $SD = 16.44$) years. In all, 21.6% were high school graduates, 59.5% had completed some college, 12.0% were college graduates, and 3.0% had graduate degrees.

Measurement

Locus of control. The study measured locus of control with Levenson's (1974) 12-item index. Respondents rated their agreement, ranging 1 (*strongly disagree*) to 5 (*strongly agree*), with items that reflect three dimensions of locus of control: powerful others control (e.g., "My life is chiefly controlled by powerful others"), chance control (e.g., "When I get what I want it's usually because I'm lucky"), and internal control (e.g., "My life is determined by my own actions"). Responses to the first two dimensions, reflecting external control, were reverse-coded. Therefore, higher scores evidenced greater internal control. This method of assessing level of locus of control has been valid and reliable in past research (e.g., Haridakis, 2002; Rubin, 1993). Responses were summed and averaged to create an internal control index ($M = 3.48$, $SD = 0.44$, $\alpha = .74$).

Self-efficacy. The self-efficacy scale used to measure respondents' perceptions of their level of political self-efficacy was adapted from prior research (e.g., Morrell, 2003; Niemi, Craig, & Mattei, 1991). Respondents rated their agreement, ranging 1 (*strongly disagree*) to 5 (*strongly agree*) with the seven items adapted from that previous research to measure perceptions of political self-efficacy, either internal (e.g., "I consider myself to be well-qualified to participate in politics") or external (e.g., "People like me don't have any say about what the government does"). Items reflecting low self-efficacy were reverse coded so that higher scores on the index represented greater political self-efficacy. Responses were summed and averaged to create the self-efficacy measure ($M = 3.13$, $SD = 0.57$, $\alpha = .67$).

Political orientation. This study measured political orientation with Mehrabian's (1996) Conservatism-Liberalism scale. This 7-item instrument was a well-suited measure in this study because it taps a person's political leanings as opposed to political affiliation. Respondents rated their agreement, ranging 1 (*strongly disagree*) to 5 (*strongly agree*), with each item. Responses were summed and averaged to create an index of political orientation ($M = 3.02$, $SD = 0.72$, $\alpha = .82$).

Influence of family and friends. Research has suggested that influence of significant others in one's life impacts political attitudes and behaviors. Influence of family and friends was measured with five items that tapped both social and behavioral influences of respondents' family and friends. Three items asked whether their parents, other family members, and friends are or were politically active. The remaining two items asked whether either or both parents encouraged the respondent to vote and whether one or both discussed politics with them when they were younger. This method of measuring the influence of family and friends was similar to, and adapted in part from, an approach that has been used in prior research to measure social influence and encouragement of parents and peers to participate in sports fanship (e.g., Gantz, Wilson, Lee, & Fingerhut, 2008). Responses to the five items, ranging 1 (*strongly disagree*) to 5 (*strongly agree*), were summed and averaged to create the index of the influence of family and friends ($M = 3.31$, $SD = 0.82$, $\alpha = .76$).

Motives for using social media for information about the presidential campaign. We measured motivation for seeking information about the campaign with a 47-item scale adapted from previous research, which was based on past measures of interpersonal communication, various media-use motives, and additional items specifically directed at online media use (Hanson & Haridakis, 2008; Papacharissi & Rubin, 2000). In addition, we included another 12 motive items specifically related to using the Web for political information (Johnson & Kaye, 2003).

Respondents were asked to indicate how much each of the 59 motive statements was like their own reasons, ranging 1 (*not at all*) to 5 (*exactly*), for using social media for political information about the campaign. Principal components factor analysis with varimax rotation was used to analyze the motive statements. Six factors, accounting for 66.69% of the total variance, were identified. Responses to items that loaded on each factor were summed and averaged to create indices of the respective viewing motives. Results of the factor analysis are summarized in Table 1.

Factor 1, *Political Evaluation*, comprised 11 items related to using the media to evaluate issues, candidates, candidates' stands on the issues, and to reach a voting decision. ($M = 3.36$, $SD = 0.86$, $\alpha = .93$). Factor 2, *Convenient Information Seeking*, comprised 8 items related to using these media because they are an easy and new way to get information; they can be used anytime; for as long as one wants; they are liked; and one can see what's out there ($M = 3.52$, $SD = .0.84$, $\alpha = .90$). Factor 3, *Entertaining Arousal*, comprised 4 items related to using these media because it is exciting, thrilling, amusing, and peps one up ($M = 2.46$, $SD = 1.06$, $\alpha = .91$). Factor 4, *Gainful Companionship*, comprised 3 items that reflected connecting with others to alleviate loneliness or get them to do something ($M = 1.71$, $SD = 0.80$, $\alpha = .82$). Factor 5, *Self Expression*, comprised 3 items that reflected using the media to give one's input, to express oneself freely, and for the enjoyment of answering others' questions ($M = 2.40$, $SD = 0.98$, $\alpha = .81$). Factor 6, *Pass Time*, comprised 3 items that reflected using these media simply to occupy one's time and when there is nothing better to do ($M = 2.63$, $SD = 1.13$, $\alpha = .86$).

Elaboration. The study used Perse and Rubin's (1990) five-item elaboration scale to tap the respondents' level of cognitive elaboration on political content about the campaign obtained from social media they used. This

TABLE 1
Primary Factor Loadings of Motives

	Factor 1	Factor 2	Factor 3	Factor 4	Factor 5	Factor 6
To see what a candidate would do if elected	.83	.22	.06	−.07	.11	.09
To see how candidates stand on issues	.78	.32	−.02	−.08	.08	−.06
To help make up my mind about how to vote in an election	.77	.23	.04	−.05	.04	.07
To help me decide about important issues	.76	.28	.09	.10	.08	−.05
To judge what political leaders are like	.75	.13	.00	−.03	.18	.20
To keep up with the main issues of the day	.74	.28	.10	−.12	.14	.05
To remind me of my candidate's strong points	.74	.13	.20	.13	.09	.01
To find out about how issues affect people like myself	.71	.21	.11	.12	.12	−.05
To judge who is likely to win an election	.66	.08	.18	.08	.25	.10
For unbiased viewpoints	.61	.20	.16	.31	.06	−.23
To enjoy the excitement of an election race	.57	.15	.39	.14	.26	−.03
Because it is easier to get information	.35	.72	.09	−.05	.08	.12
Because I can use it anytime	.27	.71	.24	−.01	.07	.20
Because it's convenient	.22	.70	.08	.07	−.06	.10
Because I can search for information for as long or as short as I want	.26	.70	.14	.08	.14	.26
To see what is out there	.34	.64	.03	.07	.27	.06
To search for information	.44	.61	.01	−.02	.12	.11
Because I just like to use it	.17	.59	.37	.08	.11	.25
Because it provides a new and interesting way to do research	.21	.59	.32	.21	.25	−.06
Because it is exciting	.19	.20	.83	.20	.19	.15
Because it is thrilling	.14	.17	.81	.26	.17	.19
Because it peps me up	.13	.13	.77	.29	.21	.15
Because it amuses me	.18	.30	.65	.08	.13	.35
So I won't have to be alone	.01	.01	.18	.82	.04	.26
Because it makes me feel less lonely	−.02	.03	.14	.79	.08	.24
Because I want someone to do something for me	.14	.00	.18	.73	.22	.12
To give my input	.26	.15	.13	.14	.81	−.00
To participate in discussions	.21	.14	.10	.10	.77	−.06
Because I can express myself freely	.15	.18	.29	.26	.62	.21
Because I enjoy answering other people's questions	.23	.03	.25	.15	.62	.25

(Continued)

TABLE 1
Continued

	Factor 1	Factor 2	Factor 3	Factor 4	Factor 5	Factor 6
When I have nothing better to do	.01	.21	.18	.24	.02	.78
Because it passes the time away, particularly when I'm bored	−.04	.23	.22	.26	.09	.77
Because it gives me something to occupy my time	.06	.25	.23	.24	.12	.71
Eigenvalue	6.78	4.43	3.39	2.85	2.73	2.50
% variance explained	19.94	13.03	9.98	8.38	8.02	7.34
M	3.36	3.52	2.46	1.71	2.40	2.63
SD	.86	.84	1.06	.80	.98	1.13
Cronbach's α	.93	.90	.91	.82	.81	.86

Note. This factor analysis was published earlier in Haridakis, P., & Hanson, G. (2010). Campaign 2008: Comparing YouTube, social networking and other media use among younger voters and older voters. In L. Kaid & J. Hendricks (Eds.), *Techno-politics and presidential campaigning: New technologies, new voices, new voters.* New York: Routledge.

TABLE 2
Summary of Beta Coefficients When Regressing Political Cynicism on Audience Individual Differences, Motives, Social Media Use and Elaboration on Political Content

	Step 1	Step 2	Step 3	Step 4	Step 5
Age	.10*	.08	.10*	.08	.05
Gender	−.15**	−.16**	−.16**	−.16**	−.16**
Education	−.11*	−.09	−.08	−.08	−.08
Political self-efficacy		−.06	−.11*	−.11*	−.14*
Locus of control		.02	−.01	−.01	−.03
Influence of family & friends		−.12*	−.14*	−.11*	−.14**
Political Orientation		−.09	−.07	−.08	−.07
Political evaluation			.06	.05	−.02
Convenient info seeking			.02	.03	−.01
Entertaining arousal			.13	.12	.12
Gainful companionship			−.16**	−.15**	−.15**
Self expression			.03	.06	.04
Pass time			.01	−.01	.01
YouTube use				.06	.05
Social network use				−.13*	−.14*
Blogging use				−.06	−.06
Elaboration					.21**

Note. $R = .19$, $R^2 = .04$, $F(3, 453) = 5.83$, $p < .01$ for Step 1; $R = .25$, $R^2 = .06$, $\Delta R^2 = .03$, $F(7, 449) = 4.35$, $p < .001$ for Step 2; $R = .31$, $R^2 = .09$, $\Delta R^2 = .03$, $F(13, 443) = 3.50$, $p < .001$ for Step 3; $R = .33$, $R^2 = .11$, $\Delta R^2 = .01$, $F(16, 440) = 3.25$, $p < .001$ for Step 4; $R = .36$, $R^2 = .13$, $\Delta R^2 = .02$, $F(17, 439) = 3.81$, $p < .001$ for Step 5.
*$p < .05$. **$p < .01$. ***$p < .001$.

index relates media content to existing knowledge and images. The items pertain to thinking about the media content and its consequences. Participants reported how often they have thoughts referenced in the five statements, ranging 1 (*never*) to 5 (*very often*). Responses to the five items were summed and averaged to create an index of cognitive elaboration ($M = 3.15$, $SD = 0.82$, $\alpha = .90$).

Amount of social media use. The study asked respondents to indicate how often (1 = *never*, 5 = *very often*) they used each of three social media sources for acquiring political information about the presidential campaign. These were YouTube or other video-sharing sites such as Google Videos; SNS such as Facebook, MySpace, or LinkedIn; and political blogs. Of these sources for political information, on average participants used YouTube or other video-sharing sites most often ($M = 2.55$. $SD = 1.41$), followed by SNS ($M = 2.04$. $SD = 1.23$) and political blogs ($M = 1.76$. $SD = 1.08$).

Cynicism. The study used Pinkleton and Austin's (2001) six-item political cynicism scale. Respondents rated their agreement, ranging 1 (*strongly disagree*) to 5 (*strongly agree*), with each item. Responses were summed and averaged to create an index of political cynicism ($M = 3.15$, $SD = 0.82$, $\alpha = .75$).

RESULTS

RQ1a, 1b, and 1c asked whether the amount of time using each of the three social media was related to political cynicism. Cynicism related significantly and negatively with social networking ($r = -.14$, $p < .01$) and blogging ($r = -.09$, $p < .05$). It was not significantly related to using YouTube ($r = -.03$, $p = .52$). Of course, the findings do not demonstrate a causal relationship, but they do suggest that the use of SNS and political blogs correlated to lower levels of self-reported voter cynicism.

Multiple regression analysis was used to examine the contributions of background characteristics; motives for using social media for political information about the campaign; how often participants used YouTube, SNS, and blogs for political information about the campaign; and cognitive elaboration to explaining political cynicism. The overall regression analyses were used to answer RQ2. Guided by the uses and gratifications model previously described, variables were entered into the equations in the following conceptual order: (a) demographics, (b) social media user background characteristics, (c) user motives, (d) amount and type of media used, and (e) elaboration on political content.

Predicting Political Cynicism

Variables entered on the first step (age, gender, education) accounted for 3.7% of the variance ($R = .19$, $p < .01$). Age ($\beta = .10$, $p < .05$), gender ($\beta = -.15$, $p < .01$), and education ($\beta = -.11$, $p < .01$) were all predictors of political cynicism. Entering other background characteristics on the second step increased explained variance by an additional 2.6%. The F change was significant ($p < .05$). Influence of family and friends ($\beta = -.12$, $p < .05$) was the only predictor. In addition, age and education ceased to be predictors at this step. Entering the motives on the third step added an additional 3% to the variance. The F change was significant ($p < .05$). Gainful companionship motivation ($\beta = -.16$, $p < .01$) was a significant negative predictor of political cynicism. Age ($\beta = .10$, $p < .05$), and political self-efficacy ($\beta = -.11$, $p < .05$) emerged as predictors at this step and gender ($\beta = -.16$, $p < .01$), and influence of family and friends ($\beta = -.14$, $p < .05$), remained predictors. Use of YouTube, SNS, and blogging were entered on Step 4. The F change was not significant ($p = .11$). But amount of time spent in social networking was a significant negative predictor ($\beta = -.13$, $p < .05$) of cynicism. Gender, political self-efficacy, influence of family and friends, gainful companionship motivation remained predictors; age ceased to be a predictor. Elaboration was entered on the fifth step. Explained variance increased by 2.3%, with a significant change in F ($p < .01$). Elaboration was a significant positive predictor ($\beta = .21$, $p < .01$).

Accordingly, after all variables were entered, gender ($\beta = -.16$, $p < .01$), political self-efficacy ($\beta = -.14$, $p < .05$), influence of family and friends ($\beta = -.14$, $p < .01$), gainful companionship motivation ($\beta = -.15$, $p < .01$), social networking ($\beta = -.14$, $p < .05$), and elaboration ($\beta = .21$, $p < .01$), were significant contributors to the final equation. The final equation accounted for 12.9% of the variance in cynicism, $R = .36$, $R^2 = .13$, $F(17, 439) = 3.81$, $p < .001$. The results of the regression analysis are listed in Table 2.

These results suggest, at least among this sample, that male individuals low in self-efficacy who elaborated on political information about the campaign, but tended not to use SNS for political information about the campaign and whose family and friends did not provide robust examples of political socialization influence from their family and friends, were more cynical than their counterparts.

DISCUSSION

The primary purpose of this study was to examine the use of new social network media during the 2008 presidential campaign and the impact of their use on political cynicism. Drawing on assumptions of uses and gratifications theory, we also considered the contribution of certain user background characteristics and motives for using social media during the campaign. The 2008 presidential election provided an important context for this exploratory study because it was the first presidential election in which these social media were readily available.

Each of the social media studied here provides users with the ability to access political information on demand, but in different ways. YouTube is a delivery system for video, SNS such as Facebook and MySpace are used primarily for interpersonal and intergroup communication, and certain political blogs provide a forum for commenting on and reading about political information in a more mass communication-related context.

The media's role in contributing to or detracting from political cynicism has been a widely studied concern in political communication research over the years. Consequently, examining the possible role of newer media sources during the first presidential campaign in which they emerge on the political media landscape is an important contribution to the literature. It permits us to consider how using their use and effects may be similar to how audiences use older media while permitting us to consider what may be new in the way they are used by audiences and the effects of that use. For example, is You-Tube simply a new video channel like TV, or does its social networking characteristics alter the effects of older generation video channels? Similarly, is Facebook simply another interpersonal or group communication channel or does its online characteristics alter the effects of other modes of interpersonal communication?

The results of this study lend support to researchers who claim that media use itself may not be a major contributor to political cynicism (e.g., Pinkleton et al., 1998). In an environment in which people have a number of media from which to choose, the most significant predictors of cynicism may reside in the individual. Among this particular group of participants, background characteristics and motives for seeking political information were important. Political self-efficacy, influence of family and friends, and the motivation to use media for gainful companionship all predicted lower levels of cynicism. In addition, and contrary to early media research in this area, the use of the medium of SNS predicted lower levels of cynicism. The only independent variable in this study to predict higher levels of cynicism was the measure of elaboration.

Implications

Political self-efficacy was a negative predictor of cynicism. This is consistent with a large body of research that has suggested that those who feel they are more politically efficacious tend not to be highly cynical of politics and campaigns (e.g., Cappella & Jamieson, 1997).

Of the background characteristics that predicted cynicism, the one that may be most fruitful to consider in future research is the influence of family and friends. The participants in this study who discussed politics and/or have been encouraged to vote by their family (items that composed this measure) tended to be less cynical. This suggests that such interpersonal and familial political socialization may lead people to be less cynical.

Prior research has suggested that the influence of one's family and friends as political socialization agents is important and contributes to one's political attitudes and behavior such as civic participation (Matthews & Howell, 2006; McDevitt & Kiousis, 2007). Similarly, researchers have found that those who engage in interpersonal conversations about politics reported lower levels of cynicism (Jasperson & Hyun Jung, 2007). If the influence is positive toward the political process, then it is reasonable to assume that one would be less cynical. Our measure of the influence of family and friends included indicators of such positive influence and interaction (e.g., being encouraged to vote by parents, discussing politics with parents, having politically active friends and family).

The importance of interpersonal communication (or at least a desire for it) may be reflected in our finding that gainful companionship—the only socially oriented motive—was a predictor. The Internet has long been regarded as a medium that is particularly amenable to interpersonal connection and social activities (e.g., Hampton & Wellman, 2003; Harasim, 1993). In particular, YouTube gives users a forum for such connection and sharing information with others (e.g., The EDUCAUSE Learning Initiative, 2006; Fernando, 2007). SNS are designed explicitly for this purpose.

Our findings linking an interpersonal motive and a lack of cynicism may support a long-standing view that interpersonal networks are used as resources for those who don't trust the conventional media (Katz & Lazarsfeld, 1955). Thus, using media that help people connect with those they know may lead them to find sources they deem to be more trustworthy than the mainstream media.

However, we should be cautious not to conclude from just one study that those who are motivated to use media for interpersonal reasons may be less cynical because gainful companionship was the weakest of the motives in the study. The fact that gainful companionship was a weak motive for seeking political information is not surprising. Political evaluation and information seeking are logically more salient reasons for desiring political information. However, the fact that gainful companionship was weaker than other motives also may simply be an artifact of the fact that this was the first election in which social media were prevalent.

Nonetheless, consistent with other research, gainful companionship does suggest a social utilitarian reason for using media generally (Hanson & Haridakis, 2008) and for political information specifically (Kaye & Johnson, 2003).

Moreover, for participants in this study, the use of SNS predicted a lower level of cynicism. This finding offers preliminary justification for considering the role of these media forms in future elections as they gain greater prominence on the media landscape. It is interesting to speculate that media that permit interaction with other citizens offer new ways to participate with others in the political process. One feature is the ability to express oneself both by creating content and by responding to others. But there may be something else about SNS that makes them important predictors of political perceptions such as cynicism. That is highlighted by the fact that political blogs, which also permit reading and commenting with others, was not related to and failed to predict cynicism. It may be that SNS are inherently more social and that blogs may be perceived as more mass-communication oriented (i.e., more likely to be read like a traditional newspaper).

Our findings beg the question, What types of social networks do these social media entail, and what are their specific relationships to cynicism? A key tenet of some of the early investigations of offline social networks is that social interaction exposes people to a different set of politically relevant information and stimuli than they possess individually (Huckfeldt, 2001; Mutz, 2002).

By the same token, the finding that use of SNS negatively predicted political cynicism must be interpreted cautiously. Although the use of some SNS may be associated with lower cynicism among some users, the small negative correlations between cynicism and YouTube use and between cynicism and social network use suggest that they may not be major inhibitors of political cynicism. Thus, a wider array of factors that may work in concert with use of these media must be considered in future research.

Finally, the strongest predictor of cynicism was elaboration. Those who elaborated on the content (e.g., thought about it over and over) tended to be more cynical than those who did not elaborate on the content. It is interesting that elaboration, a lone activity, predicted greater cynicism. However, other predictors that were more social in nature (i.e., influence of family and friends, social motivation, and use of social networking) predicted lower cynicism. These results may suggest that one way to mitigate political cynicism is through social media use.

In addition to specific background characteristics and motives, we also considered some demographic variables in this study, specifically age, education, and gender. Of these, only gender was a predictor of political cynicism. When combined with other factors, the results suggest that men who were low in self-efficacy and did not seek political information for companionship tended to be more cynical. Or, alternatively, perhaps the results suggest men who were high in self-efficacy and sought political information for gainful companionship and turned to social networking sites for that information were less cynical.

Limitations and Future Research

There were some obvious limitations to this study that should be addressed in future research. First, we applied a uses and gratifications framework in this exploratory study. Accordingly, we focused more on the role of individual differences, motives, and the selection of media for political information than on the actual content consumed. We did not assess the type or nature of the discussion that occurred on SNS. We also did not assess the actual content viewed on YouTube. Future research should consider such content-related questions.

Future research also should examine in much greater detail the contribution of personal background characteristics and motives when examining media effects. We examined specific background characteristics that prior literature suggested should be relevant to political cynicism and/or political media use. However, if as this study argues, social media give individual users enhanced opportunities to be more actively involved in content creation and distribution (one example being through the various social media sites), then the examination of the users in greater detail is not only appropriate but necessary to understand better the specific motives, levels of activity, and effects of their media use. For example, beyond elaboration, we didn't consider other aspects of activity, such as users' level of intentionality when seeking political fare. Many researchers have assumed that Internet use is more interactive than the use of older media. But, without empirical confirmation, we don't know that such speculation is necessarily correct. For example, surfing YouTube videos for political fare may be no more interactive than channel surfing for such fare on television. If use of the two channels is similar, differences in effects may be difficult to interpret.

In addition, this study did not differentiate between those who create media content in the social networking environments and those who merely read or watch the content posted by others. The interpersonal nature of social media provides researchers with an opportunity to study concepts such as opinion leadership in political campaign communication at a level that could not have been imagined in early political studies. These newer media also give researchers an exciting opportunity to consider the flow of communication in the diffusion of ideas and the mobilization of political participation.

Another obvious limitation of this study was the fact that participants were drawn from a convenience sample. Future research should solicit broader, more random samples for the purposes of generalizability. Future research also should consider the relative influence of social media use among users of traditional media vis-à-vis the influence of other media they consume. For some, the social media outlets are their primary source of news and information. For others, SNS may simply complement, and even be subservient to their use of other media such as television, newspapers, and other Internet sources.

REFERENCES

Althaus, S. L., & Tewksbury, D. (2000). Patterns of Internet and traditional news media use in a networked community. *Political Communication, 17*(1), 21–45.

Ancu, M., & Cozma, R. (2009). MySpace politics: Uses and gratifications of befriending candidates. *Journal of Broadcasting and Electronic Media, 53*, 567–583.

Armbruster, A. (2008, April 28). Local stations should be socializing; networking sites can help viewers connect to community, broadcasters. *Television Week*, p. 10.

Atkin, H. (2008, January 14). Cable news networks giving it their all; operations change to cover high-energy political campaign with keen viewer interest. *Television Week*, p. 28.

Austin, E. W., & Pinkleton, B. E. (1999). The relation between media content evaluations and political disaffection. *Mass Communication & Society, 2*, 105.

Benoit, W. L., & Hansen, G. J. (2004). The changing media environment of presidential campaigns. *Communication Research Reports, 21*, 164–173.

Berelson, B. (1966). Democratic theory and public opinion. In B. Berelson & M. Janowitz (Eds.), *Reader in public opinion and communication* (pp. 489–504). New York: The Free Press.

Bimber, B. (1998). The Internet and political transformation: Populism, community, and accelerated pluralism. *Polity, 31*, 133–160.

Bouza, F. N. (2004). The impact area of political communication: Citizenship faced with public discourse. *International Review of Sociology, 14*, 245–259.

Boyd, D. (2008). Can social network sites enable political action? *International Journal of Media & Cultural Politics, 4*, 241–244.

Brady, H. E., Verba, S., & Schlozman, K. L. (1995). Beyond SES: A resource model of political participation. *American Political Science Review, 89*, 271–294.

Brown, J., Broderick, A. J., & Lee, N. (2007). Word of mouth communication within online communities: Conceptualizing the online social network. *Journal of Interactive Marketing, 21*(3), 2–20.

Campbell, A., Gurin, G., & Miller, G. W. (1954). *The voter decides.* Evanston, IL: Row, Peterson, & Co. *As quoted in* Morrell, M. E. (2003). Survey and experimental evidence for a reliable and valid measure of internal political efficacy. *Public Opinion Quarterly, 67*, 589–602.

Campus, D., Pasquino, G., & Vaccari, C. (2008). Social networks, political discussion, and voting in Italy: A study of the 2006 election. *Political Communication, 25*, 423–444.

Cappella, J. N., & Jamieson, K. H. (1997). *Spiral of cynicism: The press and the public good.* New York: Oxford University Press.

Carr, D., & Stelter, B. (2008, November 3). Campaigns in a Web 2.0 world. *New York Times*, p. 1.

Chaffee, S. H., & Kanihan, S. F. (1997). Learning about politics from mass media. *Political Communication, 14*, 421–430.

Cohen, N. (2008, January 21). Campaign reporting in under 140 taps. *New York Times*, p. 3.

Dennis, J., & Webster, C. (1975). Children's images of the president and of government in 1962 and 1974. *American Politics Quarterly, 3*, 386–405.

de Vreese, C. H. (2005). The spiral of cynicism reconsidered. *European Journal of Communication, 20*, 283–301.

de Vreese, C. H., & Elenbaas, M. (2008). Media in the game of politics: Effects of strategic metacoverage on political cynicism. *International Journal of Press/Politics, 13*, 285–309.

Dobbin, M. (2007, September/October). Social media. *Canadian Dimension, 41*, 14.

Doddington, F., & Adams, J. (2007, November). *Evaluating Internet content relevance through active participation in social networks*. Paper presented at the annual meeting of the National Communication Association, Chicago, IL.

The EDUCAUSE Learning Initiative. (2006). *7 things you should know about YouTube* (ELI7018). Washington, DC: Author. Retrieved from http://www.educause.edu/ELI/7ThingsYouShouldKnowAboutYouTu/156821

Eveland, W. P., Jr. (2004). The effect of political discussion in producing informed citizens: The roles of information, motivation, and elaboration. *Political Communication, 21*, 177–193.

Fernando, A. (2007). Social media change the rules. *Communication World, 24*(1), 9–10.

Finkel, S. E. (1993). Reexamining the "minimal effects" model in recent presidential campaigns. *Journal of Politics, 55*(1), 1–21.

Forrest, A. L., & Weseley, A. J. (2007). To vote or not to vote? An exploration of the factors contributing to the political efficacy and intent to vote of high school students. *Journal of Social Studies Research, 31*(1), 3–11.

Gantz, W., Wilson, B., Lee, H., & Fingerhut, D. (2008). Exploring the root of sports fanship. In L. W. Hugenberg, P. M. Haridakis & A. C. Earnheardt (Eds.), *Sports mania: Essays on fandom and the meida in the 21st century* (pp. 63–77). Jefferson, NC: McFarland.

Gennaro, C. D., & Dutton, W. H. (2007). Reconfiguring friendships: Social relationships and the Internet. *Information, Communication & Society, 10*, 591–618.

Gibson, J. L. (2001). Social networks, civil society, and the prospects for consolidating Russia's democratic transition. *American Journal of Political Science, 45*(1), 51–68.

Gilliam, F. D., Jr., & Iyengar, S. (2000). Prime suspects: The influence of local television news on the viewing public. *American Journal of Political Science, 44*, 560–573.

Hampton, K., & Wellman, B. (2003). Neighboring in netville: How the Internet supports community and social capital in a wired suburb. *City & Community, 2*, 277–311.

Hanson, G., & Haridakis, P. (2008). YouTube users watching and sharing the news: A uses and gratifications approach. *Journal of Electronic Publishing, 11*. doi:10.3998/3336451.0011.305

Harasim, L. M. (1993). Networlds: Networks as social space. In L. M. Harasim (Ed.), *Global networks : Computers and international communication* (pp. 15–34). Cambridge, MA: MIT Press.

Haridakis, P. M. (2002). Viewer characteristics, exposure to television violence, and aggression. *Media Psychology, 4*, 323–352.

Ho, S., & Niederdeppe, J. (2008, May). *Mass media exposure, trust, social networks, and online health information seeking among Internet users*. Paper presented at the annual convention of the International Communication Association, Montreal, Canada.

Huckfeldt, R. (2001). The social communication of political expertise. *American Journal of Political Science, 45*, 425–439.

Hwang, H., Shah, D., & Cho, J. (2007, May). *Effects of media distrust on participatory democracy: Media distrust, democratic skepticism, and campaign participations*. Paper presented at the annual convention of the International Communication Association, San Francisco, CA.

Jackson-Beeck, M. (1979). Interpersonal and mass communication in children's political socialization. *Journalism Quarterly, 56*(1), 48–53.

Jasperson, A. E., & Hyun Jung, Y. (2007). Political advertising effects and America's racially diverse newest voting generation. *American Behavioral Scientist, 50*, 1112–1123.

Johnson, T. J., & Kaye, B. K. (2003). A boom or bust for democracy: How the Internet influences political attitudes and behaviors. *Harvard International Journal of Press/Politics, 8*(3), 9–34.

Jones, S., Millermaier, S., Goya-Martinez, M., & Schuler, J. (2008, September). Whose space is MySpace? A content analysis of MySpace profiles. *First Monday*, p. 1.

Jost, J. T., Glaser, J., & Kruglanski, A. W. (2003). Political conservatism as motivated social cognition. *Psychological Bulletin, 129*, 339–375.

Kaid, L. L. (2002). Political advertising and information seeking: Comparing exposure via traditional and Internet channels. *Journal of Advertising, 31*(1), 27–35.

Kaid, L. L., Postelnicu, M., Landreville, K., Hyun Jung, Y., & LeGrange, A. G. (2007). The effects of political advertising on young voters. *American Behavioral Scientist, 50*, 1137–1151.

Katz, E., Blumler, J. G., & Gurevitch, M. (1974). Utilization of mass communication by the individual. In J. G. Blumler & E. Katz (Eds.), *The uses of mass communications: Current perspectives on gratifications research* (pp. 19–32). Beverly Hills, CA: Sage.

Katz, E., & Lazarsfeld, P. F. (1955). *Personal influence: The part played by people in the flow of mass communications.* Glencoe, IL: Free Press.

Kaye, B. K., & Johnson, T. J. (2002). Online and in the know: Uses and gratifications of the Web for political information. *Journal of Broadcasting & Electronic Media, 46*(1), 54–71.

Kaye, B. K., & Johnson, T. J. (2003). From here to obscurity?: Media substitution theory and traditional media in an online world. *Journal of the American Society for Information Science & Technology, 54*(3), 260–273.

Kaye, B. K., & Johnson, T. J. (2004). A Web for all reasons: Uses and gratifications of Internet components for political information. *Telematics & Informatics, 21*, 197–223.

Kaye, B. K., & Johnson, T. J. (2006). The age of reasons: Motives for using different components of the Internet for political information. In A. Williams & J. C. Tedesco (Eds.), *The Internet election* (pp. 147–167). Landham, MD: Rowman and Littlefield.

Kim, J., Wyatt, R. O., & Katz, E. (1999). News, talk, opinion, participation: The part played by conversation in deliberative democracy. *Political Communication, 16*, 361–385.

Kingdon, J. (1970). Opinion leaders in the electorate. *Public Opinion Quarterly, 34*, 256–261.

Klapper, J. T. (1963). Mass communication research: An old road resurveyed. *Public Opinion Quarterly, 27*, 515–527.

Koch, J. W. (2003). Political cynicism and third party support in American presidential elections. *American Politics Research, 31*(1), 48–65.

Koch, N. S. (1994). Changing times? The effect of the *New York Times* on college students' political information and. *Social Science Journal, 31*(1), 29–39.

Landreville, K. (2007, May). *Fear, framing, and terrorism: Television news coverage of the 2004 presidential election.* Paper presented at the annual convention of the International Communication Association, San Francisco, CA.

Lange, P. G. (2007). Publicly private and privately public: Social networking on YouTube. *Journal of Computer-Mediated Communication, 13*(1), 361–380.

Lazarsfeld, P. F., Berelson, B., & Gaudet, H. (1944). *The people's choice; how the voter makes up his mind in a presidential campaign.* New York: Duell.

Learmonth, M. (2008, November 14). One-way media lost the election as cable, interactive dominated. *Advertising Age*, p. 1.

Lee, K. M. (2006). Effects of Internet use on college students' political efficacy. *CyberPsychology & Behavior, 9*, 415–422.

Leighley, J. (1996). Group membership and the mobilization of political participation. *Journal of Politics, 58*, 447–464.

Leshner, G., & McKean, M. L. (1997). Using TV news for political information during an off-year election: Effects on political knowledge and cynicism. *Journalism & Mass Communication Quarterly, 74*(1), 69–83.

Levenson, H. (1974). Activism and powerful others: Distictions within the concepts of internal–external control. *Journal of Personality Assessment, 38*, 377–383.

Levy, J. (2008). Beyond "Boxers or Briefs?": New media brings youth to politics like never before. *Phi Kappa Phi Forum, 88*(2), 14–16.

Lipset, S. M., & Schneider, W. (1983). The decline of confidence in American institutions. *Political Science Quarterly, 98*, 379–403.

Lipset, S. M., & Schneider, W. (1987). The confidence gap during the Reagan years, 1981–1987. *Political Science Quarterly, 102*, 1–23.

Makinen, M., & Kuira, M. W. (2008). Social media and postelection crisis in Kenya. *International Journal of Press/Politics, 13*, 328–335.

Matthews, T. L., & Howell, F. M. (2006). Promoting civic culture: The transmission of civic involvement from parent to child. *Sociological Focus, 39*(1), 19–35.

McDevitt, M., & Kiousis, S. (2007). The red and blue of adolescence: Origins of the compliant voter and the defiant activist. *American Behavioral Scientist, 50*, 1214–1230.

McLeod, J., & Becker, L. B. (1974). Testing the validity of gratifications measures through political effects analysis. In J. G. Blumler & E. Katz (Eds.), *The uses of mass communications: Current perspectives in gratifications research* (Vol. 3, pp. 137–163). Beverly Hills, CA: Sage.

McLeod, J. M., Scheufele, D. A., & Moy, P. (1999). Community, communication and participation: The role of mass media and interpersonal discussion in [US] local political participation. *Political Communication, 16*, 315–336.

Mehrabian, A. (1996). Relations among political attitudes, personality, and psychopathology assessed with new measures of libertarianism and conservatism. *Basic & Applied Social Psychology, 18*, 469–491.

Miller, A. H. (1974). Political issues and trust in government: 1964–1970. *American Political Science Review, 68*, 951–972.

Morrell, M. E. (2003). Survey and experimental evidence for a reliable and valid measure of internal political efficacy. *Public Opinion Quarterly, 67*, 589–602.

Moy, P., & Gastil, J. (2006). Predicting deliberative conversation: The impact of discussion networks, media use, and political cognitions. *Political Communication, 23*, 443–460.

Mutz, D. C. (2002). Cross-cutting social networks: Testing democratic theory in practice. *American Political Science Review, 96*(1), 111–117.

Newton, K. (1999). Mass media effects: Mobilization or media malaise? *British Journal of Political Science, 29*, 577–599.

Niemi, R. G., Craig, S. C., & Mattei, F. (1991). Measuring internal political efficacy in the 1988 national election study. *American Political Science Review, 85*, 1407–1413.

Ohr, D., & Schrott, P. R. (2001). Campaigns and information seeking. *European Journal of Communication, 16*, 419–449.

Ostroff, D. H., & Sandell, K. (1984). Local station coverage of campaigns: A tale of two cities in Ohio. *Journalism Quarterly, 61*, 346–351.

Palser, B. (2007, June/July). Politics 2.008. *American Journalism Review, 29*(3), 50.

Papacharissi, Z. (2009). The virtual geographies of social networks: A comparative analysis of Facebook, LinkedIn and ASmallWorld. *New Media & Society, 11*(1/2), 199–220.

Papacharissi, Z., & Rubin, A. M. (2000). Predictors of Internet use. *Journal of Broadcasting & Electronic Media, 44*, 175–196.

Perse, E. M. (1990). Media involvement and local news effects. *Journal of Broadcasting & Electronic Media, 34*(1), 17–37.

Perse, E. M., & Rubin, A. M. (1990). Chronic loneliness and television use. *Journal of Broadcasting and Electronic Media*, *34*(1), 37–53.

Pinkleton, B. E., & Austin, E. W. (2001). Individual motivations, perceived media importance, and political disaffection. *Political Communication*, *18*, 321–334.

Pinkleton, B. E., & Austin, E. W. (2002). Exploring relationships among media use frequency, perceived media importance, and media satisfaction in political disaffection and efficacy. *Mass Communication & Society*, *5*, 141–163.

Pinkleton, B. E., & Austin, E. W. (2004). Media perceptions and public affairs apathy in the politically inexperienced. *Mass Communication & Society*, *7*, 319–337.

Pinkleton, B. E., Austin, E. W., & Fortman, K. K. J. (1998). Relationship of media use and political disaffection to political efficacy and voting behavior. *Journal of Broadcasting & Electronic Media*, *42*(1), 34–50.

Pinkleton, B. E., Um, N.-H., & Austin, E. W. (2002). An exploration of the effects of negative political advertising on political decision making. *Journal of Advertising*, *31*(1), 13–25.

Price, V., Nir, L., & Cappella, J. N. (2006). Normative and informational influences in online political discussions. *Communication Theory*, *16*(1), 47–74.

Putnam, R. (2000). *Bowling alone: The collapse and revival of American community*. New York: Simon and Schuster.

Robbin, A., & Buente, W. (2008). Internet information and communication behavior during a political moment: The Iraq war, March 2003. *Journal of the American Society for Information Science & Technology*, *59*, 2210–2231.

Robinson, M. J. (1976). Public affairs television and the growth of political malaise: The case of the "selling of the Pentagon." *American Political Science Review*, *70*, 409–432.

Rotter, J. B. (1966). Generalized expectancies for internal versus external control of reinforcement. *Psychological Monographs*, *80*, 1–28.

Rubin, A. M. (1993). The effect of locus of control on communication motivation, anxiety, and satisfaction. *Communication Quarterly*, *41*, 161–171.

Ruggiero, T. E. (2000). Uses and gratifications theory in the 21st century. *Mass Communication & Society*, *3*(1), 3–37.

Schenck-Hamlin, W. J., & Procter, D. E. (2000). The influence of negative advertising frames on political cynicism and politician accountability. *Human Communication Research*, *26*(1), 53–75.

Scheufele, D. A. (2002). Examining differential gains from mass media and their implications for participatory behavior. *Communication Research*, *29*(1), 46–65.

Shah, D. V., Kwak, N., & Holbert, R. L. (2001). "Connecting" and "disconnecting" with civic life: Patterns of Internet use and the production of social capital. *Political Communication*, *18*(2), 141–162.

Spigel, L. (2009). My TV studies . . . now playing on a YouTube site near you. *Television & New Media*, *10*(1), 149–153.

The State of the News Media 2007. (2008). Washington, DC: Project for Excellence in Journalism.

Sweetser, K. D., & Kaid, L. L. (2008). Stealth soapboxes: Political information efficacy, cynicism and uses of celebrity weblogs among readers. *New Media & Society*, *10*(1), 67–91.

Sweetser, K. D., & Lariscy, R. W. (2008). Candidates make good friends: An analysis of candidates' use of Facebook. *International Journal of Strategic Communication*, *2*, 175–198.

Whitney, D. (2008, May 12). Stations put the election online: Broadcasters are turning to technology to reach younger news consumers. *Television Week*, p. 26.

Xenos, M., & Foot, K. (2007, May). *Not your father's Internet: The generation gap in online politics*. Paper presented at the annual convention of the International Communication Association, San Francisco, CA.

Did Social Media Really Matter? College Students' Use of Online Media and Political Decision Making in the 2008 Election

Matthew James Kushin
Department of Communication
Utah Valley University

Masahiro Yamamoto
The Edward R. Murrow College of Communication
Washington State University

This study examined college students' use of online media for political purposes in the 2008 election. Social media attention, online expression, and traditional Internet attention were assessed in relation to political self-efficacy and situational political involvement. Data from a Web survey of college students showed significant positive relationships between attention to traditional Internet sources and political self-efficacy and situational political involvement. Attention to social media was not significantly related to political self-efficacy or involvement. Online expression was significantly related to situational political involvement but not political self efficacy. Implications are discussed for political use of online media for young adults.

During the 2006 and 2008 election seasons, new technologies emerged that enable individuals to participate in media-rich online communities organized around the creation and exchange of media content (Kolbitsch & Maurer, 2006; O'Reilly, 2005; Rainie, 2007b; Tapscott & Williams, 2006).[1] Such social media were quite popular in the 2008 election campaign among young adults. For example, young adults used video sharing and social network sites to obtain campaign information and/or share campaign news with others, exchange their political views, and express support for a candidate (Kohut, 2008; Smith & Rainie, 2008).

As political actors used social media for their campaign, and young adults were relying less on traditional news media and more on new online media for political information (Kohut, 2008), some political and media observers commented that social media played a significant role in the 2008 campaign in affecting young voters' political cognition and behaviors (Hesseldahl, MacMillan, & Kharif, 2008; Marchese, 2008; Owen, 2008). Existing literature on the political utility of social media provides mixed evidence, however. Although some studies have uncovered its beneficial effects on political outcomes such as political efficacy and social capital (Kim & Geidner, 2008; Utz, 2009; Valenzuela, Park, & Kee, 2009), others have reported no significant linkage between social media use and political cognition and behaviors (Ancu & Cozma, 2009; Gil de Zúñiga, Puig, & Rojas, 2009; Zhang, Johnson, Seltzer, & Bichard, 2010).

The purpose of this study is to examine college students' use of online media, namely, social media attention and online expression as well as traditional Internet attention, in relation to political self-efficacy and situational political involvement in the 2008 presidential election. As political campaigns increasingly make use of these new media, it is important to understand the impact on political communication in the contemporary political environment. The present study extends previous research on the political utility of social media by introducing an expanded conception of social media with various forms of user-generated campaign information, and by conceptually differentiating and comparing cognitive and behavioral aspects of social media with traditional Internet sources.

---

[1]For example, YouTube, which was invented in 2005 and did not exist during the 2004 presidential election campaign (YouTube.com, 2010), is a video-sharing Web site that both the 2008 major party presidential candidates used to disseminate campaign video.

POLITICAL DECISION MAKING: EFFICACY AND INVOLVEMENT

Learning effective decision-making skills is a critical component to evaluating and understanding public issues (Beyth-Marom, Fischhoff, Quadrel, & Furby, 1991). Decision-making variables are particularly important in the political process, as they serve democratic theory that presumes an active and informed citizenry (Parry, Moyser, & Day, 1992; Verba & Nie, 1972; Verba, Schlozman, & Brady, 1995). These variables are useful indicators of political behavior, as direct measures such as self-report of voting often provide inaccurate pictures of citizens' political behavior (Leshner & Thorson, 2000).

Among other decision-making variables, a line of research has focused on political self-efficacy and situational political involvement (Austin & Pinkleton, 1999; Austin, Van de Vord, Pinkleton, & Epstein, 2008; Pinkleton & Austin, 2001; Pinkleton, Austin, & Fortman, 1998). Political self-efficacy is a key barometer of a healthy democracy (Craig, Niemi, & Silver, 1990). It is defined as an individual's belief that through their efforts they can impact political processes (Tan, 1980), and has been shown to be highly predictive of political participation (Scheufele & Nisbet, 2002) and voting intent or behavior (Leshner & Thorson, 2000; Pinkleton & Austin, 2001; Pinkleton et al., 1998).

Situational political involvement is defined as the perceived relevance of an issue at a given moment or the degree of interest in social situations such as an election outcome (Austin & Pinkleton, 1999; Faber, Tims, & Schmitt, 1993; Pinkleton & Austin, 2004; Salmon, 1986; Zaichkowsky, 1985). It is a psychological state "particularly important to political decision making because of its role in motivating information source use and learning" (Pinkleton & Austin, 2001, p. 322). Prior research has shown that the more an issue is perceived relevant and interesting, the greater the need for information, which increases information-oriented media use (Chew, 1994). In a political context, situational political involvement is a point of entrance into the political process as the involved voter is more motivated to seek out information, which in turn leads to knowledge gain (Tan, 1980) and voting intent (Pinkleton & Austin, 2001).

Social cognitive theory posits that one's involvement with a subject grows over time through positive personal experiences, as one increases self-efficacy (Bandura, 1997). Increases in self-efficacy further facilitate cognitive involvement and behaviors that seek to fulfill one's interest in a subject (Bandura, 1997). In this respect, situational involvement, self-efficacy, and media use are cosupportive constructs. Accordingly, citizens high in political self-efficacy report high cognitive involvement with politics (Austin et al., 2008; Pinkleton & Austin, 1998, 2001). Prior studies have examined the link between traditional news media and these decision-making variables (Austin et al., 2008; Pinkleton & Austin, 1998, 2001) paving the way for exploration into whether emergent social media platforms similarly impact political decision making.

TYPES OF ONLINE POLITICAL ACTIVITY

Existing scholarship differentiates political Internet activity into two forms (Katz, Rice, & Aspden, 2001; Shah, Cho, Eveland, & Kwak, 2005; Wang 2007). The first political activity focuses on information-seeking behaviors in which the individual gathers information by attending to Internet sources. The second political activity focuses on a more active process in which the individual interacts with others or participates in online communities. This act is conceptually different from the cognitive process of information gathering. Katz et al. (2001) termed this active behavior "interaction" such as e-mail exchange with fellow citizens or government officials and participation in online discussions. Shah et al. (2005) termed such behaviors "interactive civic messaging," consisting of interaction through e-mail. Wang's (2007) factor analysis supported these conceptual distinctions, demonstrating a two-factor model of political Internet use: information seeking and opinion expression.

To contribute to the existing literature on political Internet activity in the new media age, the present study delineates online information-seeking behavior into two components: traditional Internet sources and information sources that constitute the realm of social media (Correa, Hinsley, & Gil de Zúñiga, 2010). Specifically, the present study conceptually differentiates these components along the boundary of the main content creator. Traditional Internet sources rely predominantly on paid professionals, whereas social media rely primarily on interaction among users. To be sure, the news media and candidates publish content in the blog format and use social media tools to disseminate information or interact with the public. However, these are institutionalized communication acts in which the content producer is separate from the consumer to whom content is distributed (Bruns, 2006). Conversely, social media rely on what Bruns (2006) terms produsage, an organic production model in which boundaries between producer and consumer are eliminated such that users create the content for each other. Such communities rely on user collaboration and an ethic of openly sharing user creations (Bruns, 2006; Kolbitsch & Maurer, 2006).

The Internet and Politics

During its history, the Internet has developed into a key political information source. Between 1996 and 2008, the percentage of Americans who got political information online rose from 4% to 40% (Rainie, 2007a; Smith & Rainie, 2008). Reliance on the Internet for public affairs content has always been popular among young adults, with 37% of political Internet use in 1996 by persons younger than 30 (Rainie, 2007a).

Between the 2000 and 2006 election cycles, a number of online information sources witnessed significant growth in use such as traditional news organization Web sites, candidate Web sites, state and local government Web sites, and online news portals such as AOL and Yahoo! (Rainie, Cornfield, & Horrigan, 2005; Rainie & Horrigan, 2007). They represent established political information sources that received significant portions of the online political news traffic in the elections leading up to the 2008 election cycle (Kohut, 2008).

Social Media and Politics

The growth of online political behavior has been facilitated partly by the recent emergence of new interactive, media-rich Web sites. These Web sites, often referred to as social media, exist under the conceptual umbrella of Web 2.0. Web 2.0 Internet networks are valued in proportion to their capacity to harness the participation of online communities in the production, amalgamation, and exchange of information (O'Reilly, 2005).

Scholarship investigating social media has tended to focus predominantly on social network sites, community sites such as Facebook and MySpace that allow users to create profiles and establish connections with friends and acquaintances on the Internet (e.g., Ancu & Cozma, 2009; boyd & Ellison, 2007; Hayes, 2008; Williams & Gulati, 2007). Social network sites are a popular form of social media, whereas other formats such as blogs, microblogs, and video-sharing sites, among others, are also characterized by Web 2.0 elements. Microblogs such as Twitter allow users to post short messages that are published online in real time. Video-sharing sites such as YouTube enable users to share user-created video and interact with other users in an online community. A broader and more inclusive definition of social media is thus needed for researchers seeking to study these new media forms. For example, Correa et al. (2010) broadened this definition by adding instant messaging, a tool that enables social interaction. Scholars have also folded blogs into the social media umbrella given their function as "personal publication tools" (Gil de Zúñiga et al., 2009, p. 566) and their ability to foster interaction (Meraz, 2009). An underlying commonality is the user-generated element characterized by openness and collaboration (Bruns, 2006; Leung, 2009; Nyland, Marvez, & Beck, 2007).

As political communication sources, social media are a recent phenomenon. Nearly all major party candidates used social media during the 2008 campaign (Hayes, 2008), with some beginning their use in the 2006 midterm election (Gueorguieva, 2008). Attention to social media for campaign information was significant during the 2008 campaign, particularly among young adults (Kohut, 2008; Smith & Rainie, 2008). For example, 27% of adults younger than 30 reported obtaining campaign information from social network sites compared to 4% of adults age 30 to 39 and only 1% older than 40 (Kohut, 2008).

Online Expression and Politics

Online expression is functionally distinct from simply consuming content online (Katz et al., 2001; Shah et al., 2005; Wang, 2007). Online opinion expression and exchange have grown significantly in recent years. A recent survey indicates 15% of Americans used the Internet at least once a week during the 2008 election to urge others to support a candidate, and 10% made an online donation to a candidate or campaign (Smith & Rainie, 2008). In 2008, persons younger than 30 led the way, many of whom used the Internet to exchange political opinions and post their own political commentary (Kohut, 2008; Smith & Rainie, 2008).

Social media allow users to not only seek information but also interact with others through online expression such as posting political commentaries on blogs and social network sites and sharing multimedia commentary. Social software is about the collective and is organized around human interaction (boyd, 2007). For example, Facebook users could express themselves politically in various ways such as by making online donations, encouraging their friends to vote, and posting graphics or status updates expressing political attitudes and opinions. Twitter and blogs were used by candidates and voters alike to comment on social and political issues, share information, and encourage participation. YouTube and CNN teamed up to sponsor a debate in which candidates took questions from user-created video as opposed to a moderator, further encouraging the emergent phenomenon of user-generated political video expressions.

POLITICAL DECISION MAKING AND THE INTERNET

There are two competing perspectives of the roles of the Internet in democracy. Some consider the Internet a democratizing medium, as it can increase information access and allow citizens to voice and exchange their opinions (Morris, 1999). From this perspective, the Internet brings more citizens into the political process and may be particularly effective at engaging young people (Delli Carpini, 2000). Others are less optimistic about such potential and caution against the so-called democratization myth (McChesney, 2000; Sunstein, 2001).

Existing empirical evidence indicates that Internet use is positively associated with political outcomes including situational political involvement, political efficacy, knowledge, and participation (e.g., Austin et al., 2008; Gil de Zúñiga et al., 2009; Hardy & Scheufele, 2005; Johnson & Kaye, 2003; Kaye & Johnson, 2002; Nisbet & Scheufele, 2004; Tedesco, 2007; Xenos & Moy, 2007). Following past research, traditional Internet use for campaign information is expected to be positively related to political self-efficacy and situational political involvement.

The positive relationship between Internet use and political self-efficacy and situational political involvement may translate to social media. Past studies have reported that political use of social network sites and blogs is positively related to political efficacy, political participation, and online political behaviors such as online political discussion and online participation (Gil de Zúñiga et al., 2009; Kim & Geidner, 2008; Valenzuela et al., 2009). Attention to social media would be positively associated with political self-efficacy, because use of media-rich social media applications for political information such as microblog updates and streaming live video of campaign events would give users the perception of increased engagement with preferred candidates or parties.

Attention to social media would also be positively associated with situational political involvement, because social media offer users new channels for political information. Young adults rely heavily on friends and the Internet for political information (Wells & Dudash, 2007). Rather than merely receiving political information from traditional news media sources, users can experience politics on a more familiar, personal level through the postings of friends and acquaintances. Such experiences would make politics more accessible, bringing it into the daily lives of young adults and affecting their interest in political situations. Moreover, as social media consist primarily of user-generated content, users may be able to encounter ideas and opinions not well represented in traditional news media (Gillmor, 2006), which likely increases their interest in further information seeking.

It is also likely that online expression is positively related to political self-efficacy and situational political involvement, because of its interactive features such as interactive civic messaging and online discussion

(Moy, Manosevitch, Stamm, & Dunsmore, 2005; Shah et al., 2005). Social media create venues where users can express political views and interact with others. Political use of interactive Internet features has been shown to have a greater impact on gains in political information efficacy for young adults than simple unidirectional Internet content (Tedesco, 2007).[2] This suggests that "accomplishing interactivity on a Web site offers youth a means to engage democracy" (Tedesco, 2007, p. 1191).

Further, interactivity is seen favorably for its ability to afford greater control over information seeking (Stromer-Galley & Foot, 2002). Conversation is perceived as a valuable source of political information for the involved voter (Pinkleton, 1999). Prior research has shown that the perceived importance of conversation for obtaining campaign information predicts situational political involvement (Austin & Pinkleton, 1999). This link would extend to social media, because users can engage in political expression beyond time and space and thus have increased capacity to seek further information.

Based on the literature, the following hypotheses were formulated:

H1a: Attention to social media for campaign information will be positively associated with political self-efficacy.
H1b: Online expression about the campaign will be positively associated with political self-efficacy.
H1c: Attention to traditional Internet sources for campaign information will be positively associated with political self-efficacy.
H2a: Attention to social media for campaign information will be positively associated with situational political involvement.
H2b: Online expression about the campaign will be positively associated with situational political involvement.
H2c: Attention to traditional Internet sources for campaign information will be positively associated with situational political involvement.

METHOD

During the 2 weeks prior to the November 4, 2008, election, researchers conducted an online survey of college students at a large public

---

[2]Political information efficacy is a type of political efficacy that concerns specifically the "voter's confidence in his or her own political knowledge and its sufficiency to engage in the political process" (Kaid, McKinney, & Tedesco, 2007, p. 1096). Although it is a specific type of efficacy focused on information, it fits under the conceptual definition used in this study: an individual's belief that through their efforts they can impact political processes (Tan, 1980).

university in the Northwest. As the focus of this study is on young adults' use of social media, college students are considered an appropriate population. College students are known to be among the most Internet-connected subgroups of the population and frequent users of e-mail (Jones, 2002). Every student enrolled at the university under study had a university-assigned e-mail address. A probability-based sample of the student body was obtained via the university registrar. An invitation e-mail was sent to the e-mail address of each individual in the sample. A follow-up e-mail reminder was sent during the week before the election. The survey completion rate was 10.85%. Although this response rate is admittedly low, it is consistent with the trend of e-mail solicitation survey research (Sheehan, 2001). Two respondents, who were not 18 years old or older, were directed to the end of the survey, as they were unable to participate. Respondents who were nontraditional students and were older than 29 were removed because this study focused on young adults. Twenty-five respondents were removed for this reason, which accounted for 5.8% of the sample. The resulting sample size was 407.

Measures

Participants completed Likert-style scale items. The measures of political self-efficacy and situational political involvement were derived from past research (Austin et al., 2008; Pinkleton & Austin, 1998, 2001, 2004; Pinkleton, Um, & Austin, 2002). Using the conceptual framework previously discussed as a guide, this study examines three forms of online political activity: attention to social media for campaign information, online expression about the campaign, and attention to traditional Internet sources for campaign information. The measures of social media attention and online expression were based on popular and emerging social media platforms that served as political information traffic leading up to the 2008 campaign (Gueorguieva, 2008; Kohut, 2008; Smith & Rainie, 2008). The measures of traditional Internet sources were designed to capture established online sources of political information (Rainie et al., 2005; Rainie & Horrigan, 2007). Attention measures were used to assess the information-seeking dimension because they capture cognitive engagement with an information source, a level of cognitive expenditure not accounted for by the passive measure of exposure to, or encounter with, information (Chaffee & Schleuder, 1986).

A principal component analysis of 15 political Internet use items was conducted using direct oblimin rotation, as it was expected that political

Internet use is multidimensional and its dimensions are not orthogonal.[3] Based on the conceptual framework, a prior criterion of a three-factor solution was specified for extraction. A primary factor loading of .50 was used as a guide for determining the minimum primary loading of an item (Hair, Anderson, Tatham, & Black, 1998), and an item that loaded at .32 or higher on two or more components was considered problematic (Costello & Osborne, 2005). A three-factor solution explained 52.4% of the variance, with the three components explaining 31.47%, 12.09%, and 8.84% of the variance, respectively.

The items that were expected to load respectively on attention to social media, attention to traditional Internet sources, and online expression were indeed observed to load on each underlying component. Five of the items loaded together on the first component: personal blogs; video-sharing Web sites; microblogs; social networking Web sites; and online forums and discussion boards. These items were combined to form an *attention to social media* index ($\alpha = .78$).

Five indicators loaded together on the second component: government Web sites; candidate's Web sites; network TV news Web sites; print media news Web sites; and news pages of Internet service providers. These items were combined into an *attention to traditional Internet sources* index ($\alpha = .66$).

The final items loaded together on the third component, with the exception of participation in online discussion. The participation in online discussion item loaded moderately high on both the first and third components. Therefore, it was excluded from subsequent analysis. The remaining items were writing blog posts on political issues; creating and posting online audio, video, animation, photos, or computer artwork to

---

[3]Using a 7-point Likert-type scale with *no attention* and *a lot of attention* as anchors, respondents were asked, "For information about the election, how much attention have you been paying to each of the following?": (1) "Personal blogs," (2) "Video-sharing websites (YouTube)," (3) "Microblogs," (4) "Social networking Web sites (e.g., Facebook or MySpace)," (5) "Online forums and discussion boards." (6) "Government Web sites (e.g., local, state, or national)," (7) "Candidate's Web sites," (8) "Network TV news Web sites (e.g., CNN.com, ABCnews.com, or MSNBC.com)," (9) Print media news Web sites (e.g., *New York Times* or *US News and World Report* Web sites)," and (10) "News pages of Internet service providers (e.g., Google News or Yahoo! News)." Using a 7-point Likert-type scale with *none* and *a lot* as anchors, respondents were also asked, "In regard to the election, how much have you engaged in each of the following?": (11) "Writing blog posts on political issues," (12) "Creating and posting online audio, video, animation, photos or computer artwork to express political views," (13) "Sharing political news, video clips, or others' blog posts online," (14) "Participating in online political discussions (e.g., Discussion boards and chat rooms), and (15) "Exchanging opinions about politics via e-mail, social networking Web sites, microblogging (such as Twitter) or instant messenger."

express political views; sharing political news, video clips, or others' blog posts online; and exchanging opinions about politics via e-mail, social networking Web sites, microblogging, or instant messenger. The *online expression* index, hence, consists of the four items ($\alpha = .75$).

Political self-efficacy.   Political self-efficacy was measured by four items using a 7-point Likert-type scale with *strongly disagree* and *strongly agree* as anchors. Respondents were asked, "Please indicate whether you strongly disagree or strongly agree with each of the following statements": (1) "My vote makes a difference," (2) "I have a real say in what the government does," (3) "I can make a difference if I participate in the election process," and (4) "Voting gives people an effective way to influence what the government does." These items were combined into an additive index ($\alpha = .89$), with a higher score indicating higher political self-efficacy.

Situational political involvement.   Situational political involvement was measured by four items using a 7-point Likert-type scale with *strongly disagree* and *strongly agree* as anchors. Respondents were asked, "Please indicate whether you strongly disagree or strongly agree with each of the following statements": (1) "I pay attention to election information," (2) "I like to stay informed about the elections," (3) I'm interested in election information, and (4) "I actively seek out information concerning the elections." These items were summed into an additive index ($\alpha = .89$), with a higher score indicating higher situational political involvement.

To examine the unique influence of the three online media variables, several variables were used as controls including age, sex, political ideology, and traditional news media use (i.e., newspapers, television, magazine, and radio). Sex was coded with women as the high value (53.3%). Due to the overwhelming percentage of respondents who identified as White (88.2%), race was not included in the present analysis (see Table 2). Although the majority of the respondents were White, these statistics do not differ significantly from the student population at the university used in the survey. Household income also was not used in the analysis, as a large number of respondents opted out of answering this question, which may have been a result of confusion, as many college students remain dependent on their parents' income and thus may not have found this question applicable. Not using these variables is consistent with previous research which has examined the political lives of young adults (Kaid et al., 2007). Traditional news media variables were measured by asking respondents, on a 7-point scale, how much attention they paid to each of the following for information about the election: newspapers, network television news, magazines, and radio.

TABLE 1
An Analysis of Types of Political Internet Activity

	Attention to social media	Attention to traditional internet sources	Online expression
Microblogs	**.771**	−.116	−.099
Personal blogs	**.764**	−.097	−.083
Video-sharing Web sites	**.710**	.082	.169
Online forums and discussion boards	**.673**	−.192	.019
Social networking Web sites	**.637**	.067	.153
TV news Web sites	.120	**.700**	−.272
Print media news Web sites	.040	**.678**	−.041
News pages of Internet service providers	.106	**.663**	.136
Candidate's Web sites	−.079	**.549**	−.268
Government Web sites	−.139	**.513**	−.272
Creating and posting online audio, animation, photos, or computer artwork to express political views	−.175	.076	**−.812**
Writing blog posts on political issues	.126	.023	**−.681**
Sharing political news, video clips, or others' blog posts online	.305	−.008	**−.612**
Participating in online political discussions	.403	−.133	−.569
Exchanging opinions via e-mail, social networking sites	.209	.143	**−.534**

Note. Bold text indicates significant factor loadings.

TABLE 2
Sample Demographics

	M or % (N)	SD
Gender		
Male	44.2% (180)	
Female	53.3% (221)	
Age	21.5	2.65
Ethnicity[a]		
White	88.2% (359)	
African American	2.9% (12)	
Hispanic	3.4% (14)	
Asian American	7.1% (29)	
Native American	3.2% (13)	
Other	6.4% (26)	
Stance on political spectrum[b]	3.27	1.1

Note. $N = 407$.
[a]Category sums to greater than 100% because respondents of mixed ethnic background were able to select multiple criteria for ethnicity.
[b]1 = Very Conservative, 5 = Very Liberal.

To test the hypotheses, two regression models were constructed predicting political self-efficacy and situational political involvement. To counteract specification error and therefore inaccurate coefficient estimates, control variables were entered in the first block, followed by attention to social media, online expression, and attention to traditional Internet sources in the second block.

RESULTS

Table 3 shows a regression model predicting political self-efficacy. Sex ($\beta = .13$) was a significant predictor, with female respondents more politically efficacious. Radio news attention ($\beta = .11$) was a significant predictor, with respondents who attended more to radio election news being more politically efficacious. The other news attention variables—newspapers, TV news, and magazines—were not significantly related to political self-efficacy. These variables accounted for 9.6% of the variance in political self-efficacy.

The first set of hypotheses stated that attention to social media, online expression, and attention to traditional Internet sources would be positively associated with political self-efficacy. H1a and H1b were not supported, as

TABLE 3
Predicting Political Self-efficacy and Situational Political Involvement

	Political self-efficacy β	Situational political involvement β
Age	−.04	.11*
Sex (female)	.13**	−.06
Political ideology	−.01	−.02
Newspaper attention	−.04	.12*
TV news attention	.10	.08
Radio attention	.11*	.04
Magazine attention	−.03	−.14**
R^2 (%)	9.6***	12.9***
Attention to social media	.06	−.00
Online expression	.08	.16**
Attention to traditional Internet sources	.33***	.38***
Block R^2 (%)	11.1***	15.7***
Total R^2 (%)	20.6***	28.6***

Note. Cell entries are final standardized regression coefficients.
*$p < .05$. **$p < .01$. ***$p < .001$.

attention to social media and online expression were not significantly related to political self-efficacy. Attention to traditional Internet sources was positively related to political self-efficacy ($\beta = .33$), indicating that above and beyond all other variables, respondents who paid greater attention to traditional Internet sources for campaign information were more politically efficacious than those who paid less attention. This lends support to H1c. The three online media variables as a whole explained 11.1% of the total variance.

Table 3 also presents a regression model predicting situational political involvement. Age ($\beta = .11$) was positively associated with situational political involvement, with older respondents being more involved in the election. Newspaper attention ($\beta = .12$) was a significant predictor of situational political involvement, with those with greater attention to newspapers for campaign information being more involved in the election. Magazine attention ($\beta = -.14$) was negatively associated with situational political involvement. These variables accounted for 12.9% of the variance.

The second set of hypotheses predicted that attention to social media, online expression, and attention to traditional Internet sources would be positively associated with situational political involvement. H2a was not supported, as attention to social media was not significantly related to situational political involvement. H2b and H2c were supported. Online expression and attention to traditional Internet sources were significant predictors of situational political involvement ($\beta = .16$ and $\beta = .38$, respectively). That is, respondents who frequently expressed opinions about the election online and those who paid greater attention to traditional Internet sources for campaign information were respectively more involved in the election. The three online media variables explained 15.7% of the total variance.

DISCUSSION

Traditional Internet Sources

Scholars have argued that the Internet is a democratizing medium for its capacity to provide increased access to information and interaction, bringing individuals into the political process (Delli Carpini, 2000; Morris, 1999). A competing perspective suggests the Internet is a polarizing medium that allows like-minded individuals to share and reinforce their preexisting political beliefs (Ancu & Cozma, 2009; Sunstein, 2001). Our results support the former. The results are consistent with prior research that has shown the positive effects of the Internet on democracy (e.g., Johnson & Kaye, 2003; Kaye & Johnson, 2002; Nisbet & Scheufele, 2004; Tedesco, 2007).

The present analysis showed a moderate link between attention to traditional Internet sources for campaign information and political self-efficacy and situational political involvement. Consistent with past survey reports (Kohut, 2008; Smith & Rainie, 2008), this finding suggests that the Internet is an important political information source for young adults. Of importance, attention to radio was the only significant predictor of political self-efficacy, and attention to newspapers was the only significant predictor of situational political involvement. These results may suggest that traditional news media are becoming less important in the political lives of young adults. Alternatively, young adults may be moving to online editions of traditional news media including portal Web sites such as Yahoo! and MSN that cull stories from them. When considered in this way, traditional news media are not necessarily becoming less important for young adults. Rather, young adults may be using traditional news media information in online spaces. This may explain why attention to traditional Internet sources for campaign information was positively associated with political self-efficacy and situational political involvement, whereas most of the traditional news media variables were not.

Of interest, attention to social media, online expression, and attention to traditional Internet sources, as a whole, accounted for more variance in political self-efficacy and situational political involvement than demographic variables, political ideology, and traditional news media variables combined. In both cases, the new media variables accounted for more than 10% of the variance. These results also can be seen as a reflection of the prominence that Internet media have in the political lives of young adults.

Social Media

Attention to social media was expected to be positively related to political self-efficacy and situational political involvement as media-rich interaction between citizens and political actors on social media afford users the perception of increased engagement with the campaign. Also, social media allow users to experience politics at a more intimate interpersonal level and obtain user-generated political information they might not be able to obtain in traditional news sources. Indeed, young adults used social media sites like YouTube, Facebook, Twitter, and blogs to get political content and commentary from other members of the social media community as well as to get information from news sources and campaigns.

Our results did not support this reasoning. Attention to social media for campaign information was not significantly associated with political self-efficacy and situational political involvement. The nature of social media might be related to these nonsignificant effects. The relative newness of social media might have inhibited any effect on political self-efficacy and situational political involvement in the 2008 election. As can be suggested from a prior report (Smith & Rainie, 2008), users might not have been knowledgeable about social media platforms from which they could acquire accurate political information.

Although consumption of political information on social media may help cultivate the perception of increased engagement with political systems, certain types of content may inhibit this capacity. For example, political content with strong partisan or cynical messages from peers may act to offset its potentially beneficial effects on political self-efficacy, as a recent report shows that those who obtain news online tend to prefer nonpartisan sources (Purcell, Rainie, Mitchell, Rosenstiel, & Olmstead, 2010). It is also possible that some content seeking to persuade users to be more involved in the election interfered with the ability of social media to cultivate a positive sense of engagement with politics. Some might have perceived such messages as meddling, whereas others might have perceived that they were less politically prepared than their peers. Thus, it is likely that political content on social media plays the paradoxical role of exposing individuals to greater content while insulating them from gains in political self-efficacy.

The Pew Internet and American Life Project reported that many young adults do not actively search for political information but rather encounter such information while going online for other purposes (Kohut, 2008). Such unintended encounters can occur frequently in social media (Utz, 2009). Facebook and Twitter, for example, deliver a stream of status updates by other users they friend or follow. These services push content to the user with limited active information seeking. If attention to social media for political information is not as purposive as some might expect, the unintended receiving of political content may not serve to activate users' motivation to seek out information. In a related vein, the social media formats that present a wide variety of information simultaneously may distract users' attention and impair their capacity to extract politically efficacious information and seek out additional political information.

The present study contributes to a growing body of evidence that may lead scholars to question the political utility of social media (e.g., Ancu & Cozma, 2009; Gil de Zúñiga et al., 2009; Zhang et al., 2010). Despite the positive outlook expressed in political and social arenas, the information-seeking dimension of social media did not appear to play a major role in the 2008 election as it was not related to political self-efficacy and situational political involvement, important predictors of political participation (Pinkleton & Austin, 2001; Pinkleton et al., 1998).

Online Expression

Social media such as Facebook, blogs, Twitter, and YouTube offer young adults opportunities for written and multimedia political expression and interaction with others. Such interactive features of social media were expected to be related to an increased sense of political engagement and motivation to seek out information about the election. Our results showed that online expression was significantly related to situational political involvement but not political self-efficacy. This indicates that a desire to express what one has learned is connected to a desire to learn about the election. As young adults go online to express opinions, discuss issues, or share information, they become more cognitively involved in the election. This is consistent with prior studies reporting the positive effects of online political discussion in democracy (e.g., Hardy & Scheufele, 2005) and extends previous research reporting the link between perceived importance of political conversations and situational political involvement (Austin & Pinkleton, 1999).

The reasons for the nonsignificant relationship between online expression and political self-efficacy are not entirely clear. It might be that political information individuals obtain through online interaction lacks perceived credibility. As online political discourses often contain uncivil elements (Davis, 1999; Hill & Hughes, 1998), online political communication might not always be pleasant and efficacious. Further, the extent to which online content generation is gratifying is an important variable in determining its impact on general self-efficacy (Leung, 2009). The link between online expression and political self-efficacy, if any, might depend on the nature of interaction, quality of information, and extent to which it is gratifying, rather than the expression act itself. It is also important to point out that the present study examined only the effects of online expression on political self-efficacy. It is possible that the two are related in a reverse order, with those who are political efficacious more likely to engage in online expression than their counterparts.

LIMITATIONS

The present study is limited in several key respects. First, social media are constantly evolving, and the boundaries between the cognitive and behavioral aspects as well as those between social media and traditional Internet sources may become less distinct as new applications are developed and implemented. Therefore, future studies should continue to explore the dimensionality of political Internet use.

The findings must be interpreted with caution, as they are based on a college student sample and hence not generalizable to young adults in the United States. Also, the survey response rate was unfavorably low. Although the demographics of respondents were similar to the population parameters of the university, this might have produced biased estimates. The reasons for the low response rate are not entirely clear. Respondents were contacted twice, initially and right before the election, to increase the response rate for the Web survey (Kaplowitz, Hadlock, & Levine, 2004; Manfreda & Vehovar, 2008). It might be due to other sources of survey nonresponse such as the use of incentives and the timing of the follow-up contact (Lynn, 2008; Manfreda & Vehovar, 2008). At any rate, due to this limitation, the present findings should not be considered as conclusive.

Third, political involvement can be viewed as consisting of cognitive and behavioral aspects. The present study assessed a cognitive aspect of political involvement conceived as the motivation of the individual to seek out information about the election. Future research should test whether social media play a role in affecting behavioral aspects of involvement such as political participation and voting.

Finally, the present study does not draw any causal inferences about the relationships between political Internet use and political decision making because of the nature of the analysis. Longitudinal data of young adults' social media use would allow for better assessments of the political utility of online media.

CONCLUSION

These limitations and considerations notwithstanding, this study has extended prior research by offering an expanded conception of social media and by differentiating and comparing the cognitive and behavioral dimensions with traditional Internet sources. Despite popular discussion about social media as political forces in the 2008 election, traditional Internet sources played a greater role in affecting political self-efficacy and situational political involvement for the present sample.

This, of course, does not mean that social media will not play any important role in young adults' political lives. It enables various forms of interaction with fellow citizens and political actors that were not possible prior to its growth. User-generated content can provide meaningful information that citizens might not be able to acquire elsewhere. Also, its open and collaborative nature can lower the barriers of entry into politics, particularly for less politically sophisticated groups. It must be noted, however, that social media alone would not have profound and lasting effects on young adults' political decision making. It is ultimately a platform supported by users' active participation in content creation. It is thus important to educate and socialize young adults toward the political use of social media. Such socialization may increase motivated use of social media for political purposes and lead to the realization of its political benefits.

It took multiple election cycles for the public to adopt the Internet as a political information source. The same pattern of growth may be observed for social media. As can be suggested by diffusion of innovations theory (Rogers, 1995), social media are characterized by their relative advantages for political actors and citizens. Moreover, the open and participatory nature is compatible with fundamental democratic values. As the social system recognizes the utility of social media for political communication and young adults become more familiar and comfortable with using social media for political purposes, social media may become part of their political information repertoire. Research on social media is a growing line of inquiry. Further examination is required to better understand their impacts on political decision making as they develop and become more widely adopted.

REFERENCES

Ancu, M., & Cozma, R. (2009). Myspace politics: Uses and gratifications of befriending candidates. *Journal of Broadcasting & Electronic Media*, *53*, 567–583.

Austin, E. W., & Pinkleton, B. E. (1999). The relation between media content evaluations and political disaffection. *Mass Communication & Society*, *2*, 105–122.

Austin, E. W., Van de Vord, R., Pinkleton, B. E., & Epstein, E. (2008). Celebrity endorsements and their potential to motivate young voters. *Mass Communication & Society*, *11*, 420–436.

Bandura, A. (1997). *Self efficacy: The exercise of control*. New York: W. H. Freeman.

Beyth-Marom, R., Fischhoff, B., Quadrel, M. J., & Furby, L. (1991). Teaching decision making to adolescents: A critical review. In J. Baron & V. Brown (Eds.), *Teaching decision making to adolescents* (pp. 19–60). Hillsdale, NJ: Erlbaum.

boyd, d. (2007). The significance of social software. In T. N. Burg & J. Schmidt (Eds.), *Blog talks reloaded: Social software research & cases* (pp. 15–30). Norderstedt, Germany: Books on Demand.

boyd, d., & Ellison, N. (2007). Social network sites: Definition, history, and scholarship. *Journal of Computer-Mediated Communication*, *13*, 210–230.

Bruns, A. (2006). Towards produsage: Futures for user-led content production. In F. Sudweeks, H. Hrachovec, & C. Ess (Eds.), *Proceedings cultural attitudes towards communication and technology* (pp. 275–284). Perth, Australia: Murdoch University.

Chaffee, S. H., & Schleuder, J. (1986). Measurement and effects of attention to media news. *Human Communication Research*, *13*(1), 76–107.

Chew, F. (1994). The relationship of information needs to issue relevance and media use. *Journalism Quarterly*, *71*, 676–688.

Correa, T., Hinsley, A. W., & Gil de Zúñiga, H. (2010). Who interacts on the Web?: The intersection of users' personality and social media use. *Computers in Human Behavior*, *26*, 247–253.

Costello, A. B., & Osborne, J. W. (2005). Best practices in exploratory factor analysis: Four recommendations for getting the most from your analysis. *Practical Assessment, Research & Evaluation, 19*(7), 1–9.

Craig, S., Niemi, R. C., & Silver, G. E. (1990). Political efficacy and trust: A report on the NEWS pilot study items. *Political Behavior, 12,* 289–314.

Davis, R. (1999). *The Web of politics: The Internet's impact on the American political system.* Oxford, UK: Oxford University Press.

Delli Carpini, M. X. (2000). Gen.com: Youth, civic engagement, and the new information environment. *Political Communication, 17,* 341–349.

Faber, R. J., Tims, A. R., & Schmitt, K. G. (1993). Negative political advertising and voting intent: The role of involvement and alternative information sources. *Journal of Advertising, 22,* 67–76.

Gil de Zúñiga, H., Puig, E., & Rojas, H. (2009). Weblogs traditional sources online & political participation: An assessment of how the Internet is changing the political environment. *New Media & Society, 11,* 553–574.

Gillmor, D. (2006). *We the media: Grassroots journalism by the people, for the people.* Sebastopol, CA: O'Reilly Media.

Gueorguieva, V. (2008). Voters, MySpace, and YouTube: The impact of alternative communication channels on the 2006 election cycle and beyond. *Social Science Computer Review, 26,* 288–300.

Hair, J. F., Jr., Anderson, R. E., Tatham, R. L., & Black, W. C. (1998). *Multivariate data analysis* (5th ed.). Upper Saddle River, NJ: Prentice Hall.

Hardy, B. W., & Scheufele, D. A. (2005). Examining differential gains from Internet use: Comparing the moderating role of talk and online interactions. *Journal of Communication, 55,* 71–84.

Hayes, R. (2008, November). *Providing what they want and need on their own turf: Social networking, the web, and young voters.* Paper presented at the National Communication Association Annual Conference, San Diego, CA.

Hesseldahl, A., MacMillan, D., & Kharif, O. (2008, November 5). The vote: A victory for social media, too. *Business Week.* Retrieved from http://www.businessweek.com/technology/content/nov2008/tc2008115_988160.htm

Hill, K. A., & Hughes, J. E. (1998). *Cyberpolitics: Citizen activism in the age of the Internet.* Lanham, MD: Rowman & Littlefield.

Johnson, T. J., & Kaye, B. K. (2003). A boost or bust for democracy: How the Web influenced political attitudes and behaviors in the 1996 and 2000 presidential elections. *Harvard International Journal of Press/Politics, 8*(3), 9–34.

Jones, S. (2002, September 15). The internet goes to college: How students are living in the future with today's technology. *Pew Internet & American Life Project.* Retrieved from http://www.pewinternet.org/pdfs/PIP_College_Report.pdf

Kaid, L. L., McKinney, M. S., & Tedesco, J. C. (2007). Introduction: Political information efficacy and young voters. *American Behavioral Scientist, 50,* 1093–1111.

Kaplowitz, M. D., Hadlock, T. D., & Levine, R. (2004). A comparison of Web and mail survey response rates. *Public Opinion Quarterly, 68,* 94–101.

Katz, E. J., Rice, R. E., & Aspden, P. (2001). The Internet, 1995–2000: Access, civic involvement, and social interaction. *American Behavioral Scientist, 45,* 405–419.

Kaye, B. K., & Johnson, T. J. (2002). Online and in the know: Uses and gratifications of the web for political information. *Journal of Broadcasting and Electronic Media, 46,* 54–71.

Kim, Y., & Geidner, N. W. (2008, May). *Politics as friendship: The impact of online social networks on young voters' political behavior.* Paper presented at the annual meeting of the

International Communication Association, Montreal, Quebec, Canada. Retrieved from http://www.allacademic.com/meta/p233811_index.html

Kohut, A. (2008, January 11). Social networking and online videos take off: Internet's broader role in campaign 2008. *The Pew Research Center for the People and the Press*. Retrieved from http://www.pewinternet.org/pdfs/Pew_MediaSources_jan08.pdf

Kolbitsch, J., & Maurer, H. (2006). The transformation of the web: How emerging communities shape the information we consume. *Journal of Universal Computer Science, 12*, 187–213.

Leshner, G., & Thorson, E. (2000). Overreporting voting: Campaign media, public mood, and the vote. *Political Communication, 17*, 263–278.

Leung, L. (2009). User-generated content on the internet: An examination of gratitifications, civic engagement and psychological empowerment. *New Media & Society, 11*, 1327–1347.

Lynn, P. (2008). The problem of nonresponse. In E. D. de Leeuw, J. J. Hox & D. A. Dillman (Eds.), *International handbook of survey methodology* (pp. 35–55). New York: Erlbaum.

Manfreda, K. L., & Vehovar, V. (2008). Internet surveys. In E. D. de Leeuw, J. J. Hox & D. A. Dillman (Eds.), *International handbook of survey methodology* (pp. 264–284). New York: Erlbaum.

Marchese, J. (2008, January 8). Social media's election effect. *Online Spin*. Retrieved from http://www.mediapost.com/publications/?fa=Articles.showArticle&art_aid=73844

McChesney, R. (2000). *Rich media, poor democracy: Communication politics in dubious times*. New York: The New Press.

Meraz, S. (2009). Is there an elite hold? Traditional media to social media agenda setting influence in blog networks. *Journal of Computer Mediated Communication, 14*, 682–707.

Morris, D. (1999). *Vote.com: How big-money lobbyists and the media are losing their influence and the internet is giving power to the people*. Los Angeles: Renaissance Books.

Moy, P., Manosevitch, E., Stamm, S., & Dunsmore, K. (2005). Linking dimensions of internet use and civic engagement. *Journalism and Mass Communication Quarterly, 82*, 571–586.

Nisbet, M. C., & Scheufele, D. A. (2004). Political talk as a catalyst for online citizenship. *Journalism & Mass Communication Quarterly, 81*, 877–896.

Nyland, R., Marvez, R., & Beck, J. (2007). *Myspace: Social networking or social isolation?* Paper presented at the Association for Education in Journalism and Mass Communication Midwinter Conference, Reno, NV.

O'Reilly, T. (2005, September 30). *What is web 2.0: Design patterns and business models for the next generation of software*. Retrieved from http://www.oreillynet.com/pub/a/oreilly/tim/news/2005/09/30/what-is-web-20.html?page=1

Owen, S. (2008, November 3). Citizens, media use social media to monitor election. *PBS*. Retrieved from http://www.pbs.org/mediashift/2008/11/citizens-media-use-social-media-to-monitor-election308.html

Parry, G., Moyser, G., & Day, N. (1992). *Political participation and democracy in Britain*. London: Cambridge University Press.

Pinkleton, B. E. (1999). Individual motivations and information source relevance in political decision making. *Mass Communication & Society, 2*, 65–80.

Pinkleton, B. E., & Austin, E. W. (1998). Media and participation: Breaking the spiral of disaffection. In T. J. Johnson, C. E. Hays & S. P. Hays (Eds.), *Engaging the public: How government and the media can reinvigorate American democracy* (pp. 75–86). Lanham, MD: Rowman & Littlefield.

Pinkleton, B. E., & Austin, E. W. (2001). Individual motivations, perceived media importance, and political disaffection. *Political Communication, 18*, 321–334.

Pinkleton, B. E., & Austin, E. W. (2004). Media perceptions and public affairs apathy in the politically inexperienced. *Mass Communication & Society, 7*, 319–337.

Pinkleton, P. E., Austin, E. W., & Fortman, K. K. J. (1998). Relationships of media use and political disaffection to political efficacy and voting behavior. *Journal of Broadcasting & Electronic Media, 32,* 34–49.

Pinkleton, B. E., Um, N., & Austin, E. W. (2002). An exploration of the effects of negative political advertising on political decision making. *Journal of Advertising, 31,* 13–25.

Purcell, K., Rainie, L., Mitchell, A., Rosenstiel, T., & Olmstead, K. (2010, March 1). Understanding the participatory news consumer: How internet and cell phone users have turned news into a social experience. *Pew Research Center, Pew Internet & American Life Project, and Project for Excellence in Journalism.* Retrieved from http://www.pewinternet.org/Reports/2010/Online-News.aspx

Rainie, L. (2007a, May 18). E-citizen planet. *Pew Internet & American Life Project.* Retrieved from http://www.authoring.pewinternet.org/~/media/Files/Presentations/2007/2007%20-%205.18.07%20-%20The%20Internet%20and%20Politics%202007.pdf

Rainie, L. (2007b, January 31). 28% of online Americans have used the internet to tag content: Forget Dewey and his decimals, internet users are revolutionizing the way we classify information—and make sense of it. *Pew Internet & American Life Project.* Washington, DC: Pew Trusts. Retrieved July 26, 2009, from http://www.pewtrusts.org/uploadedFiles/wwwpewtrustsorg/Reports/Society_and_the_Internet/PIP_Tagging.pdf

Rainie, L., Cornfield, M., & Horrigan, J. (2005, March 6). The Internet and Campaign 2004. *Pew Internet & American Life Project.* Retrieved from http://www.pewinternet.org/~/media//Files/Reports/2005/PIP_2004_Campaign.pdf.pdf

Rainie, L., & Horrigan, J. (2007, January 17). Election 2006 online. *Pew Internet & American Life Project.* Retrieved from http://www.pewinternet.org/~/media/Files/Reports/2007/PIP_Politics_2006.pdf.pdf

Rogers, E. M. (1995). *Diffusion of innovations* (4th ed.). New York: Free Press.

Salmon, C. T. (1986). Perspectives on involvement in consumer and communication research. In B. Dervin & M. J. Voigt (Eds.), *Progress in communication sciences, Volume VII* (pp. 243–268). Norwood, NJ: Ablex.

Scheufele, D. A., & Nisbet, M. C. (2002). Being a citizen online: New opportunities and dead ends. *Harvard Journal of Press/Politics, 7*(3), 55–75.

Shah, D. V., Cho, J., Eveland, W. P., Jr., & Kwak, N. (2005). Information and expression in a digital age: Modeling internet effects on civic participation. *Communication Research, 32,* 531–565.

Sheehan, K. B. (2001). E-mail survey response rates: A review. *Journal of Computer-Mediated Communication, 6*(2). doi:10.1111/j.1083-6101.2001.tb00117.x

Smith, A., & Rainie, L. (2008). The Internet and the 2008 election. *Pew Internet & American Life Project.* Washington, DC: Pew Trust. Retrieved form http://www.pewinternet.org/pdfs/PIP_2008_election.pdf

Stromer-Galley, J., & Foot, K. (2002). Citizen perceptions of online interactivity and implications for political campaign communication. *Journal of Computer Mediated Communication, 8*(1). doi:10.1111/j.1083–6101.2002.tb00161.x

Sunstein, C. R. (2001). *Republic.com.* Princeton, NJ: Princeton University Press.

Tan, A. S. (1980). Mass media use, issue knowledge and political involvement. *Public Opinion Quarterly, 44,* 241–248.

Tapscott, D., & Williams, A. D. (2006). *Wikinomics: How mass collaboration changes everything.* New York: Penguin.

Tedesco, J. C. (2007). Examining Internet interactivity effects on young adult political information efficacy. *American Behavioral Scientist, 50,* 1183–1194.

Utz, S. (2009). The (potential) benefits of campaigning via social network sites. *Journal of Computer-Mediated Communication, 14,* 221–243.

Valenzuela, S., Park, N., & Kee, K. F. (2009). Is there social capital in a social network site?: Facebook use and college students' life satisfaction, trust, and participation. *Journal of Computer-Mediated Communication, 14*, 875–901.

Verba, S., & Nie, N. H. (1972). *Participation in America: Political democracy and social equality.* New York: Harper and Row.

Verba, S., Schlozman, K. L., & Brady, H. E. (1995). *Voice and equality: Civic voluntarism in American politics.* Cambridge, MA: Harvard University Press.

Wang, S. (2007). Political use of the internet, political attitudes and political participation. *Asian Journal of Communication, 17*, 381–395.

Wells, S. D., & Dudash, E. (2007). Wha'd'ya know? Examining young voters' political information and efficacy in the 2004 election. *American Behavioral Scientist, 50*, 1280–1289.

Williams, C. B., & Gulati, G. J. (2007). *Social networks in political campaigns: Facebook and the 2006 midterm elections.* Paper presented at the annual meeting of the American Political Science Association, Chicago, IL. Retrieved from http://www.bentley.edu/news-events/pdf/Facebook_APSA_2007_final.pdf

Xenos, M., & Moy, P. (2007). Direct and differential effects of the Internet on political and civic engagement. *Journal of Communication, 57*, 704–718.

YouTube.com. (2010). *About YouTube.* Retrieved from http://www.youtube.com/t/about

Zaichkowsky, J. L. (1985). Measuring the involvement construct. *Journal of Consumer Research, 12*, 341–352.

Zhang, W., Johnson, T. J., Seltzer, T., & Bichard, S. (2010). The revolution will be networked: The influence of social networks on political attitudes and behaviors. *Social Science Computer Review, 28*, 75–92.

APPENDIX

Measures and
Indexes

	M	SD	*Cronbach's* α
Political self-efficacy	18.56	5.67	.89
Situational political involvement	22.78	4.66	.89
Newspaper attention	4.63	1.83	
TV news attention	4.51	1.90	
Radio attention	3.13	2.06	
Magazine attention	2.89	1.87	
Attention to social media	10.74	6.09	.78
Attention to traditional Internet sources	19.70	6.53	.66
Online expression	7.79	5.03	.75

The 2008 Presidential Election, 2.0: A Content Analysis of User-Generated Political Facebook Groups

Julia K. Woolley and Anthony M. Limperos
College of Communications
The Pennsylvania State University

Mary Beth Oliver
Department of Film/Video & Media Studies
The Pennsylvania State University

Although Facebook is primarily known for building and maintaining relation-ships, the 2008 presidential election highlighted this social networking website as a viable tool for political communication. In fact, during primary season until Election Day in 2008, Facebook users created more than 1,000 Facebook group pages that focused on Barack Obama and John McCain. Using quan-titative content analysis, the primary purpose of this study was to assess how both John McCain and Barack Obama were portrayed across these

Facebook groups. Results indicated that group membership and activity levels were higher for Barack Obama than for John McCain. Overall, Barack Obama was portrayed more positively across Facebook groups than John McCain. In addition, profanity, racial, religious, and age-related language were also coded for and varied with regard to how each candidate was portrayed. Theoretical and practical implications are discussed.

Social media went from being virtually unknown in the realm of politics to a budding form of political communication during the 2008 presidential election. Although previous presidential elections have shown us that candidates' own Web sites are important for fund-raising and communicating directly with supporters, the 2008 presidential election showed us that social media (e.g., Facebook, Twitter, and blogging) have become increasingly popular forums for political participation (Quily, 2008; A. Smith, 2009; Vitak et al., 2009). Over the past decade, online social networking sites such as Facebook and MySpace have experienced unparalleled success. Currently, Facebook has more than 500 million users worldwide, is second to only Google in terms of worldwide Internet traffic, and has emerged as the most widely used form of social networking (Alexa, 2010; Facebook Press Room, 2010).

Whereas Facebook is essentially a social networking Web site that allows users to present an array of interpersonal information about themselves through a variety of Web 2.0 modalities and technologies, the use of Facebook during the 2008 presidential election showed that it has vitality as a political communication tool. In fact, the use of Facebook for political purposes was so significant that it caused major news organizations like CNN to pose the question, "Will the 2008 presidential election be won on Facebook?" (Rawlinson, 2007). Although it may be too soon to assess the total impact of Facebook on the 2008 presidential election, the fact that it is now widely used in the political process gives rise to many theoretical and practical questions about its utility, especially with regard to user-generated content.

Broadly, the focus of this research is to understand and describe the content of user-generated political Facebook groups. It is well known that politicians view social networking as a legitimate form of publicity and that they use it accordingly. Although candidates' own pages are interesting to study in and of themselves, we can assume that in terms of content, they are very similar to what might be delivered to the media from that particular candidate's campaign. But what happens when political content and messages are generated by ordinary citizens?

Facebook groups are one of the most used applications available on the social networking platform (Facebook, 2010). Leading up to the 2008 elections, many stories involving support groups for presidential candidates were featured on the national news. Most notably, Farouk Olu Aregbe, a college-educated Nigerian immigrant employed as a student government adviser at the University of Missouri, started the Facebook group "One Million Strong for Barack" (Vargas, 2007). Even though Aregbe was not a member of Obama's campaign team, the group that he started and managed had more than 850,000 members by the time the presidential elections took place in November. Although no statistics exist with regard to how many user-generated political Facebook groups were created during the 2008 presidential election, using the search function within Facebook revealed that more than 1,000 groups had been created for each of the two major party political candidates John McCain and Barack Obama by Election Day in 2008.

Although one can assume that these Facebook groups are important to politics based on numbers alone, little is known about how much these user-generated groups are used and for what purposes. This leads to a couple of broad questions: To what extent do user-generated political Facebook groups facilitate political discourse? Do most groups portray political candidates in a positive or negative light? As a context for political discussion, Facebook may be used as a powerful tool for mobilizing groups, managing one's self-image, or entertaining oneself. Although Facebook groups may be a persuasive technology with unique democratic potential, they may also serve as a forum for inflammatory conversation.

In addition to being an arena for social networking and political action, Facebook may also serve as a forum for political entertainment. In this regard, we should consider the potential impact of political messages as they are portrayed in Facebook groups. Schemas about race, religion, and age, for example, may be primed by Facebook group titles or pictures, which may serve both a persuasive function in the election itself and a longer term function in reinforcing or building stereotypes. Extant research on media portrayals of race (e.g., Mastro & Greenberg, 2000; Oliver, 1994), gender (e.g., Stern & Mastro, 2004; Vestweber, 1992), age (e.g., Lee, Carpenter, & Meyers, 2007; Peterson & Ross, 1997; Roy & Harwood, 1997), and religion (e.g., Brocket & Baird, 2008; Hill, Hickman, & McLendon, 2001; Stout & Buddenbaum, 2003; Yao, 2007) has consistently demonstrated both the disproportionate nature of negative portrayals in the media and negative effects of such portrayals in experimental contexts (e.g., Ford, 1997; Mckenzie-Mohr & Zanna, 1990). Analyzing Facebook content and the extent to which it adheres to such portrayals may both indicate how pervasive such stereotypes are in social media and serve as a first step to future studies of the effects of such portrayals.

Content analyses of prime-time television and video games have also focused on the prevalence of profanity and vulgarity, due to concerns over the media's potential to desensitize individuals to objectionable content

(Ivory, Williams, Martins, & Consalvo, 2009; Kaye & Sapolsky, 2004). Although online political discourse may differ from video games and television in many ways, the concern about content is the same. If Facebook groups are emerging as a legitimate form of political discourse, then the presence of objectionable or profane content within these groups could cheapen this discourse or impact the users of this content in unintended ways.

The aim of this study was to assess the type of content within Facebook groups of the two major party presidential candidates, John McCain and Barack Obama. First, we were interested in how group membership and activity levels differed between groups focused on different candidates. Second, we were interested in how these groups differed in terms of the valence of candidate references; use of racial, religious, and age-related references; and the presence of profanity. Based on these analyses, we offer a descriptive and theoretical account of the dominant themes stemming from the user-generated content within Facebook groups during the 2008 presidential election.

LITERATURE REVIEW

Building Community While Campaigning: The Uses of Facebook Groups

When Facebook was originally launched, it was exclusively available to college students. In 2007, Facebook amended their restrictive practices and currently allows anyone with a valid e-mail address to be a part of the Facebook community, although Facebook membership is still predominately composed of college students (Creamer, 2007; Inside Network, 2010). The purpose of Facebook is to build and facilitate online communities and social ties. For instance, a student at a large university can be affiliated with both his or her school and his or her hometown simultaneously. Although the broad community building idea is the standard on Facebook, users can also build subaffiliated communities within the Facebook community through the use of Facebook groups. A Facebook group can be created by anyone in the Facebook community and essentially allows users who share similar beliefs, interests, and ideas the ability to organize and congregate in a virtual space. The topic and purpose of such groups vary greatly, from support for nonprofit organizations, to pop-culture fan clubs, to groups which are self-declared as "totally pointless." These groups can be public or private and can have open or invitation-only access. Recently, Park, Kee, and Valenzuela (2009) found that college students often use Facebook groups for socializing, entertainment, self-status seeking, and informational purposes, and that this informational utility was correlated with higher offline civic and political engagement. These results suggest at the very least that students obtain and use political information from Facebook groups.

Facebook Groups and Politics

Westling (2007) reported that Facebook groups usually encompass a variety of topics, but some of the most prominent areas of interest often involve support for political candidates or particular positions on salient issues such as abortion. Even though Facebook groups are mainly generated by common community members, there have been instances where advertisers, advocacy groups, and politicians have created or been given access to Facebook groups. For example, during the 2006 midterm elections, the creators of Facebook gave all U.S. congressional and gubernatorial candidates access to a Facebook page, which the candidates could then personalize and make available to possible voters and supporters (Williams & Gulati, 2007). Although these pages were used by a majority of the midterm election candidates, Sweetser and Lariscy (2008) found that they were mainly used to disseminate information and that candidates themselves rarely answered any messages shared by supporters. Similarly, Bortree and Seltzer (2009) found that environmental advocacy groups often use social networking spaces to send out information but they that rarely use these platforms for two-way communication. This may be one important way that user-generated political groups differ from those that are sanctioned by formal entities such as candidates themselves or advocacy groups.

Even though there has been little empirical work published thus far that assesses if this widespread use of Facebook was effective, anecdotal evidence seems to suggest that using Facebook is beneficial in the campaign process (Smith, 2008). Campaign Web sites first appeared in the late 1990s, and the subsequent proliferation of the Internet has furthered the utility of tools like social media to disseminate political discourse. Research has shown that approximately 75% of voters younger than age 30 get half of their political information from the Internet (Jones & Fox, 2009). Generally speaking, the idea of using the Internet to connect with younger demographics of voters is not new. Although television is still the primary source through which people obtain political information, recent research has suggested that the Internet may be more effective for delivering political information to more people, especially younger demographics. For example, Kaid and Postelnicu (2005) experimentally tested for differences in attitudes toward John Kerry and George Bush following exposure to political advertising delivered through the Internet versus television. Results of the study indicated that students had more favorable attitudes toward John Kerry when they viewed his Internet advertisement rather than his television spot, whereas differences in responses to the George Bush spots were not significant based on medium. Even though these results suggest that certain candidates might perform better when given certain channels, they suggest, at the very least, that Internet is an important conduit for political communication.

This finding is both suggestive and prescriptive of the reasons why political candidates are seeking mediated technologies to deliver their messages, and may also explain why many are using the Internet to propel their own political beliefs and feelings. The capabilities of political Facebook groups are similar to those of blogs, which have been widely employed by political candidates. In 2004, democratic primary candidates utilized blogs in order to send more personalized messages to their constituents (Trammell, Williams, Postelnicu, & Landreville, 2006). However, it is important to note that campaign blogs are often managed by campaign workers and not the actual political candidates themselves.

Although there has been a lot of research that has attempted to explain the effectiveness and power of mediated political transmissions by analyzing politically sponsored blogs (e.g., Kaid & Postelnicu, 2005; Trammell et al., 2006), considerably less research attention has been given to user-generated content appearing in social networking venues. However, since the initial Facebook sponsored "Election Pulse" project that allowed politicians to have their own political groups in 2006, there has been an explosion in the number of politically oriented user-generated Facebook groups. These groups are unique because they are often not sponsored by political candidates themselves, are subscribed to by many potential voters, and vary widely in terms of their messages and scope.

While attempting to assess the effectiveness of the Facebook-sanctioned political candidate sites from the 2006 midterm elections, Williams and Gulati (2007) offered this insight:

> Selecting an actual subset of political groups was very cumbersome and challenging because candidates were hard to locate among all of the other political groups—Moreover, many of the political groups were only loosely related to politics and government or had names that were inappropriate, making it more difficult for the legitimate groups to stand out or be taken seriously. (p. 5)

Based on this insight, it is apparent that user-generated political groups are making it more difficult to decipher sanctioned political candidate groups from those that are created by laymembers of the Facebook community.

Moreover, it is widely unknown whether these user-generated political groups are being created for legitimate campaign purposes or strictly as a form of social enhancement or entertainment.

Online Impression Formation: The Impact of Web 2.0 Technologies

Should we be concerned about the differences that may exist between user-generated political Facebook groups and those which are sponsored by political candidates? Because it appears that young people are using Web 2.0 technologies like Facebook to both gather and disseminate political information, it is important to review literature involving both the salient communicative aspects and some of the potential negative effects of computer-mediated communication (CMC). Long before the commercial genesis of Internet communication technologies, the primary belief of many scholars was that CMC was far inferior to that of face-to-face communication because it did not have the ability to carry nonverbal and other social-context cues (Daft & Lengel, 1984; Rice, 1993; Short, Williams, & Christie, 1976).

Social information processing theory (Walther, 1992, 1996) was the first contemporary theory to suggest that people could decipher useful relational information through computer-mediated means that were similar to or better than traditional face-to-face interactions. Generally, the research involving social information processing theory has consistently shown that the lack of cues in CMC settings causes people to be more selective about the information they present. The selective information presented in CMC contexts often causes the receivers of these cues to overattribute similarity or dissimilarity to the sender of the message because this information serves as the only point of reference for the interacting parties (Walther, 1993, 1996). Because the purpose of the Facebook sanctioned political groups is to advance candidates' positions, it can be assumed that campaign workers go through a process to ensure that a particular group or page is representative of the candidates' desired image.

The characteristics of Facebook groups are such that individuals can present a wide variety of information about their support or discontent for a cause, issue, or candidate, and research has shown that more information often leads to a more favorable impression than limited amounts of information in online contexts (Tanis & Postmes, 2003). Even though Facebook groups have a wide variety of uses, it appears that one of the most salient reasons that people use them is to enhance their profiles (Boyd & Ellison, 2007). Accordingly, because political groups may enhance the richness of social information provided to fellow users, they may influence how people form impressions and perceive one another. Facebook may thus also function as a uniquely persuasive technology, given this salient peer influence in both viewing and joining groups.

Although CMC has been heralded for its ability to connect people in ways that are not normally possible in face-to-face interactions, it is also thought to have some negative effects. For example, the freedom of users to present any type of information they want has been identified as a mechanism for increased instances of antisocial Internet behavior, which is widely known as "flaming" (Walther, Anderson, & Park, 1994). According to O'Sullivan and Flanagin (2003),

> The process of "flaming" includes the intentional creation, transmission, and interpretation of a message that is perceived from multiple perspectives as violating norms, and which can itself be the beginning of the norm, negotiation, evolution, and realignment process. (p. 85)

If a specific user-generated political Facebook group is negatively valenced toward a particular candidate, this process can be viewed as a simple expression of disagreement or a potential attempt to try to coerce or organize individuals for a new cause. Papacharissi (2004) analyzed political discussion boards and found that although discussion within these boards was often intense, it allowed people to disagree in a way that has strong democratic potential. Although mediated political transmissions might include more instances of disagreement and possibly flaming, it is still unclear whether these messages might add to or detract from the democratic process.

Political Facebook Groups and Effects of Political Messages

In addition to those theoretical perspectives regarding the technological affordances of social networking sites as a medium for self-presentation and computer-mediated political communication, traditional media effects theories may guide our understanding of both the psychological effects of political content on Facebook as well as the motivations that may guide users' generation of such content. As mentioned earlier, political Facebook groups may serve a variety of functions. Facebook users may turn to such groups both as a forum for expressing one's political opinion and a source for gathering information about candidates. This latter use may be of particular interest given that this information is delivered in the context of a social networking site. Given the subjective importance of the opinions of those in one's peer network, Facebook groups may potentially be quite powerful in their effects on users' perceptions of candidates and relevant issues.

The presentation of these opinions may mirror the dominant frames presented by other forms of mass media. In particular, theories of content effects on viewers may apply in new and interesting ways to the generation of content in this interactive media context. Analyzing political Facebook group content through such a lens may lead to insight as to how these perspectives can be applied or adapted in reference to these new user-driven technologies. For example, one potential influence on user-generated content may be the "false consensus effect," or the idea that most of the people in the population share one's point of view (Marks & Miller, 1987). For example, if one indeed perceives that others in their network share their political leanings, then one might present more explicitly worded group names than if they were unsure about how their group would be received.

Views expressed in political Facebook groups also may reflect similar topics and themes as those that have been perpetuated in other media venues, as a result of both first- and second-order agenda setting (McCombs, 2004), priming (Iyengar & Kinder, 1987) and framing (Schufele, 1999). In this sense, the news agenda that has been shaped by old media outlets may be carried out by users in the new media context. In particular, Facebook groups may reflect themes about race, religion, and age that have been salient in the dominant discourse. Such user-generated content may similarly continue to emphasize frames relating to the private lives of the candidates and candidate likeability, which have been quite salient in the televisual medium (Johnston & Kaid, 2002). Alternatively, Facebook may serve a unique function in countering those dominant themes and discourses, in terms of the salient issues in this election regarding presidential candidates, particularly in terms of race, religion, and age.

RATIONALE AND RESEARCH QUESTIONS

The 2008 election was unique and historical in many ways. Numerous media accounts have supported the idea that Barack Obama and his campaign absolutely dominated the political landscape in terms of Internet use to garner campaign support (Baumann, 2008; Cary, 2009; Miller, 2008). Although assessing how effective each aspect of the Internet (e.g., social-networking, campaign contributions, grass roots support, etc.) was for each candidate could be gauged in terms of monetary contributions to each candidates' campaign, the focus of this research is to understand the content, group membership, and activity of user-generated, politically motivated Facebook groups. First and foremost, we were interested in understanding the overall image (whether it be positive or negative) of each of the major party presidential candidates (Barack Obama and John McCain) across their cumulative user-generated Facebook groups. Because the anonymity and freedom to post any type of information often elicit practices of online flaming (Walther et al., 1994), our research questions were also concerned with how the prevalence of profane, age-, religious-, and race-related references varied by candidate.

Although there is no real way to assess how much a particular political Facebook group is being used by its members, group size and group activity are two accessible features of groups that act as a proxy for how much activity there is for a particular group. For example, a Facebook group with 100 new members and a total group size of 4,000 would be considered to be relatively active when compared with a group that has 2 new members and only 100 total members. Accordingly, we were also interested in understanding how the valence of portrayals for each candidate varied by group size and activity. Based on the given rationale, the following research questions were proposed:

RQ1: How do groups focused on McCain versus Obama differ in terms of group membership and group activity?

RQ2: How do groups focused on McCain versus Obama differ in terms of the frequency of positive and negative references to candidates, the use of profanity, and references to race, religion and age?

RQ3: Do references to McCain versus Obama differ in terms of positive and negative comments, and positive and negative references to race, religion and age?

METHOD

This study used quantitative content analysis to evaluate the content of user-generated political Facebook groups of either John McCain or Barack Obama to describe the portrayal of each candidate and assess how those portrayals varied by group membership and activity. In order to assess the total number of political Facebook groups associated with each of the presidential candidates for the 2008 presidential election, the specific search terms "John McCain" and "Barack Obama" were entered into the advanced group search box function embedded on Facebook.com. The "Barack Obama" search produced 541 affiliated political groups, and the "John McCain" search yielded 536 affiliated political groups. Upon further examination of the search results, it became clear that they were sorted in descending order according to group membership. For example, the first group affiliated with Barack Obama had approximately 874,174 members. The second group had 222,288 members, followed by the third affiliated group, which had 87,257 members. This same pattern emerged with the John McCain search results. In sum, the search results show the most populated groups first and those that are less populated follow in descending order.

Sample

As a result of our preliminary search results, we employed a multistage sampling technique that was both purposive and systematic. In the first stage, we selected the top four Facebook groups for each candidate. Even though these groups represented less than 1% of the entire population of the groups for each candidate, it was necessary to include them because of their membership numbers. For the remaining 537 Obama groups and 532 McCain groups, respectively, we employed a systematic sampling technique with a step interval. After the purposive sample of the first 4 groups, every fourth search result was selected for analysis. We employed this technique to capture a representative sample of all the remaining groups. Because our research questions were interested in differences between political Facebook groups with large and small numbers of membership, this technique also allowed us a broad-enough sample to capture both types of groups and the potential nuances between them. Unfortunately, Facebook groups do not contain information that allows users to decipher when they are created and when they no longer exist. Because this is the case, the sampling frame for our project was subject to potential change.

To exert control over the content that we analyzed, we searched and archived all of the sampled search results and group pages by using functions built into the Mozilla Firefox Web browser. Accordingly, we captured all of the group pages at the same time on November 3, 2008, the last possible day for groups to change/add information and members before Election Day. By doing this, it ensured that all of the coded material was consistent. In all, our sample consisted of 278 total groups (Obama, $n = 139$; McCain, $n = 139$) and represented approximately 26% of the total population for all groups associated with both candidates ($N = 1077$) and 26% of the total group population per candidate. There were four cases in which the .htm files were corrupted, and these four cases were dropped from the analyses.

There were two main units of analysis that we were interested in employing: the search results pages and the actual group pages. For instance, the first search result for "Barack Obama" was a group titled "Barack Obama (One Million Strong for Barack)." The first unit of analysis was the thumbnail picture and group description on the search results page. The second unit of analysis was the actual group page. Access to the group page is obtained by clicking on the thumbnail picture in the search results page. To answer our research questions, we constructed extensive content categories that reflected and accounted for variables associated with the political Facebook search pages and groups.

Content Categories

Each group thumbnail and main group page in the sample was coded. Each coder first recorded the search term (John McCain or Barack Obama) and the entire group name for that candidate. Then, the number of group members and new group activity were recorded. After that, all group information (e.g., the group title, group picture, group description, and recent news sections) was coded for the presence or absence of a particular candidate's name and whether that particular piece of group information portrayed the candidate in a positive or negative light. In accordance with the codebook, messages coded as "positively valenced" demonstrated a favorable attitude toward the candidate, whereas messages coded as "negatively valenced" demonstrated an unfavorable attitude toward the candidate. For example, the group title "John McCain for President" was coded as a positive reference to John McCain, whereas the group title "Barack Obama wont [sic] salute my flag, and has no business being our President" was coded as a negative reference to Barack Obama. The same definition applied in categorizing the pictures. For example, a picture capturing John McCain mid-grimace was coded as "negatively valenced," whereas a standard campaign photo was coded as "positively valenced." In all cases, coders could classify any aspect of the group page as containing both positive and negative elements.

The presence of profanity, racial, religious, and age-related language, as well as the valence of that language, was also coded. For example, a group description might read, "John McCain is too old to run the country." This would be coded as a negative reference toward John McCain, which involved negative age-related language. A description reading, "Barack Obama is the antichrist," would be coded as a negative reference to Barack Obama, which involved religious language. Messages coded as profane included statements such as, "John McCain is a piece of shit" and "Fuck Barack Obama."

Most content was thus coded for the presence or absence of a particular candidate's name; the presence of any specific type of language; and then whether that piece of information was positive, negative, or both. Two of the authors of this article served as coders for the project. To calculate intercoder reliability, we used Hayes's and Krippendorf's alpha macro (Hayes & Krippendorf, 2007). Intercoder reliabilities ranged from $\alpha = .78$ to $\alpha = 1.00$. The average reliability of those content categories where coders did not reach perfect agreement was $\alpha = .90$.

Variable Creation

After coding the Facebook groups, we created new variables to use in our analyses. The first step was to determine which candidate was the primary focus of the group (in many cases, a group referenced more than one candidate throughout the page, often positively referencing one and negatively referencing the other). Thus, *Candidate Focus* was determined based upon two criteria. First, we tallied whether a candidate was referenced in the title, picture, description, and recent news sections (for a potential total of four references per candidate) and determined which candidate was referenced more often. Then, we assessed whether the candidate referenced most often throughout the page was also the only candidate referenced in the group's title. In all but nine cases, the candidate referenced most often throughout the page was also the sole candidate referenced in the title; thus Candidate Focus was easy to determine for all but these nine cases.

For the five cases in which only one candidate was mentioned in the title, but the candidates were mentioned equally often throughout the page, Candidate Focus was determined according to which candidate was mentioned in the title. In three cases, both candidates were mentioned in the title and both were mentioned equally often throughout the page. Given that the infrequency of these types of groups employing equal mention of both candidates would prohibit systematic analyses, these three cases were excluded from further analyses involving the Candidate Focus variable. In one case (titled, "No matter which Democrat gets nominated, its [sic] better than John McCain"), the candidate who was mentioned in the title (John McCain) was not the candidate who was mentioned more often throughout the page (Barack Obama). Due to the difficulty categorizing this group, the case was also excluded from further analysis involving the Candidate Focus variable. This procedure resulted in equal-sized groups of candidate focus, with 136 pages per candidate.

To compute *Positive References*, we tallied whether there were any positive candidate references in the title, picture, description, and recent news sections. To compute *Negative References*, we tallied whether there were any negative candidate references in the title, picture, description, and recent news sections. It should be noted that both of these distributions were nonnormal, and thus nonparametric procedures were used in all analyses involving these variables. For those pages that contained at least one positive or negative reference, we also created variables that indicated whether a positive reference was referring to McCain (*Positive McCain*) or Obama (*Positive Obama*), and whether a negative reference was referring to McCain (*Negative McCain*) or Obama (*Negative Obama*). There were only four cases in which positive references were made to both candidates and three cases in which negative references were made to both candidates.

The measures of *Profanity, Race, Religion,* and *Age* were computed in a similar manner, by tallying the presence of each type of reference in the title, picture, description, and recent news. Again, due to nonnormality of the distributions, nonparametric procedures were used in analyzing these variables. We then created variables that indicated whether a race, religion, or age reference was positive or negative and whether it referred to McCain or Obama (e.g., *Race Positive McCain, Race Positive Obama*). There were no instances in which references of the same type and valence were made to both candidates in a single page.

Group Activity was created as a sum of the number of posted items, videos, photos, discussion topics, and wall posts and ranged from 0 to 61,911 ($M = 443.41$, $SD = 4064.01$). *Group Membership* was simply the number of members reported by Facebook, ranging from 27 to 874,714 ($M = 5763.95$, $SD = 55004.70$). Both of these distributions were severely nonnormal, and thus nonparametric procedures were used in tests involving these measures.

RESULTS

RQ1 and RQ2 asked if groups focused on McCain versus Obama differed on a number of different variables: group membership; group activity; frequency of positive and negative references to candidates; the use of profanity; and references to race, religion, and age. Because many of these variables were substantially skewed, Mann-Whitney U-tests were employed to examine differences between McCain- and Obama-focused groups. Table 1 shows the results of these analyses.

Obama-focused groups were significantly higher than were McCain-focused groups in terms of both the number of group members and the overall level of activity. Likewise, Obama-focused pages featured a higher number of positive references and a lower number of negative references. Obama-focused pages also contained a higher number of references to race, whereas McCain-focused pages featured a significantly greater number of instances of profanity. The groups did not differ in terms of the frequency of references to religion or age.

RQ3 asked if references to McCain versus Obama differed in terms of positive and negative comments, per se, and positive and negative references to race, religion, and age. Because references to none, one, or both candidates could appear in a given Facebook group, each group was coded for the number of references for each candidate. Hence, comparisons between references to McCain versus Obama were not independent. Normally such comparisons might be analyzed via paired *t* tests, though in this instance

TABLE 1
Average Membership, Activity Level, and References as a Function of Group Focus

	Focus of group		
	McCain M (SD)	Obama M (SD)	U
No. of group members	1350.12 (7766.90)	10344.37 (77852.76)	2788.00***
Activity level	264.26 (2185.94)	635.04 (5365.87)	4550.50***
Positive references	1.83 (1.55)	2.77 (1.36)	5985.50***
Negative references	1.54 (1.38)	0.66 (1.27)	5856.50***
Profanity	0.13 (.37)	0.05 (.28)	8578.00*
Racial references	0.10 (.38)	0.28 (.57)	7882.00***
Religious references	0.15 (.41)	0.30 (.70)	8626.50
Age references	0.24 (.66)	0.12 (.37)	8806.00

Note. Because many of these variables were severely non-normal, Mann–Whitney U tests were employed to examine differences by group focus.
$^*p < .05$; $^{***}p < .001$.

variables were severely nonnormal, and in some cases contained very low frequencies. As a consequence, nonparametric procedures were employed using exact tests (Mehta & Patel, 1996). In the case of comparisons of frequencies, Wilcoxon tests were employed, and in the case of comparisons of prevalence, McNemar tests were employed. Further, because references to race, religion, and age were infrequent, these analyses compared positive and negative references to each candidate within each category only among the Facebook groups that had at least one reference of that type. Table 2 shows the results of these analyses.

Both in terms of frequency and prevalence, there were significantly more positive references and fewer negative references to Obama than to McCain. Further, there were significantly more negative references pertaining to age for McCain than for Obama. Although no other significant differences were obtained, there are several aspects of these analyses that are worthy of note. First, several comparisons were not analyzed due to the absence of references for one of the candidates (i.e., positive racial and age references to McCain). Likewise, although some of the comparisons did not reach statistical significance, this lack of significance may reflect low levels of frequency overall, and hence reduced power. For example, in terms of religion, 26.19% of all references to religion were negative references toward McCain, compared with 40.48% toward Obama. However, these differences were not statistically significant, perhaps due to the relative infrequency with which religion was referenced ($N = 40$).

TABLE 2
Frequency and Prevalence of Positive and Negative References to McCain Versus Obama

	Positive references			Negative references		
	McCain	*Obama*	*p*	*McCain*	*Obama*	*p*
Positive/Negative references[a]						
Average no. of references/ page	0.87 (1.41)	1.44 (1.66)	***	0.73 (1.25)	0.39 (0.97)	**
% with 1 reference or more	30.88%	47.43%	**	27.94%	18.75%	*
Racial references[b]						
Average no. of race references/page	0.00 (00)	0.65 (0.70)[c]		0.23 (0.62)	0.30 (0.52)	ns
% with 1 race reference or more	0%	52.50%		15.00%	27.50%	
Religious references[d]						
Average no. of religious references/page	0.07 (0.26)	0.21 (0.61)	ns	0.38 (0.73)	0.86 (1.18)	ns
% with 1 religious reference or more	7.14%	14.29%		26.19%	40.48%	
Age References[e]						
Average no. of age references/page	0.00 (0.00)	0.03 (0.17)[c]		0.91 (1.06)	0.03 (0.17)	***
% with 1 age reference or more	0%	2.94%		55.88%	2.94%	***

Note. Because these data were severely nonnormal and involved unbalanced responses, non-parametric procedures for related samples were employed, using two-tailed exact tests in the calculation of all significance levels (Mehta & Patel, 1996). Numbers in parentheses are standard deviations.
[a]$N = 272$.
[b]$N = 40$.
[c]Significance tests were not conducted due to cells with zero frequencies.
[d]$N = 42$.
[e]$N = 34$.
$^*p < .05.$ $^{**}p < .01.$ $^{***}p < .001.$

DISCUSSION

Social media stormed onto the scene as a viable political communication tool in almost viral fashion during the 2008 presidential election. Although there were many different social media venues for individuals to express their political beliefs and garner support for their candidate of choice, political Facebook groups emerged as an influential forum for political expression. Many news organizations confirmed that the Obama campaign used the Internet more effectively than the McCain camp during the election season. Although these news stories might be accurate in terms of money raised online and measurement of traffic to a particular candidates' website, they did little to describe the types of messages that were being produced by ordinary citizens through the use of social media, making studies such as this very important.

Although social media have been identified as open forums that can potentially lead to participation in the democratic process, support for this view is somewhat mixed in this investigation. In line with major media reports, groups focused on Barack Obama were more actively used, had higher group membership, and were more positive than groups featuring John McCain. Furthermore, across all groups, significantly more of the positive references referred to Obama, whereas significantly more of the negative references referred to McCain. Although there were Facebook groups that did contain race-related, age-related, or religious language, the general prevalence of these types of variables were low across groups. Of those that did contain race-related language, these references were more likely to occur in Obama-focused than McCain-focused groups. Of those groups that contained negative references to age, these references were more likely to refer to McCain than Obama. The presence of such references could be reflective of the dominant themes on Facebook but more plausibly reflect themes that were prevalent in mainstream media at the time. Finally, although the prevalence of profanity was low, the odds of there being profanity were much higher for McCain-focused groups than Obama-focused groups. These results, coupled with the fact that groups in general more negatively portrayed McCain, suggest that both supporters *and* detractors of McCain used profane language.

Overall, the most significant finding here is not just that Barack Obama seemed to have more positive support than John McCain within Facebook groups but that groups which featured McCain were overwhelmingly negative. Although this might not be surprising given the fact that younger demographics of people more heavily supported Obama, it leads to greater questions about the use of social media as a tool for promoting dialogue between people of different political allegiances. Overall, these findings may suggest that people are using Facebook groups to gather rather than share information, or possibly as a mere token gesture of support for a certain candidate or publication of their political allegiances.

The likelihood of McCain-focused groups to contain more negative and less positive references than Obama-focused groups could be explained in several ways. First, it may be a signal of the success of Obama's reported attempts to run a "positive" campaign. Alternatively, given both the relative prevalence of negative references to McCain and the general "negativity" of McCain-focused groups, this may be an indication of some frequency of "anti-McCain" Facebook groups, although this possibility was not explicitly accounted for in the current coding scheme. Finally, this discrepancy in valence between groups could be reflective of the tone and temperament of McCain supporters. In this instance, differences between groups may be reflective of discrepancies between Obama and McCain supporters in perceived social capital, particularly to the extent that such differences may drive motivations for political Facebook group use (Shah, Kwak, & Holbert, 2001). Banning (2006), for example, found that Republicans "have a significantly greater third-person perception level than Democrats" (p. 785), whereas literature on hostile media effects similarly suggests that Republicans more consistently perceive hostile media coverage as opposed to Democrats (e.g., Lee, 2005). Previous studies have demonstrated that one possible consequence of third-person perceptions of media coverage is increased voter turnout and political participation (Banning, 2006; Golan, Banning, & Lundy, 2005). Online political participation via Facebook groups may similarly result from users' reactions to unfavorable mass media portrayals of their candidate of choice, or favorable portrayals of his or her opponent, and may similarly divide along party lines. Such a reactive response may be more pronounced among those of one political leaning over another. Without further research, there is no real way to tell what the motives behind content might be, but third-person and hostile media perceptions are two possible explanations.

Social Media: Further Polarization of Politics

In the books *Republic* and *Republic 2.0*, Cass Sunstein (2001, 2007) broadly cautioned that the Internet might not be a panacea of democracy but instead might be rife with polarizing viewpoints. The results of this study suggest that although social media do indeed provide individuals a platform to express their beliefs, these expressions are often partisan and polarizing. Because Facebook is primarily used by younger people, this may not be a surprise. However, as Facebook membership increases and the platform becomes increasingly political, Republican and other party candidates will have to figure out how to increase their presence within Facebook. This movement will likely be driven by how well campaigns are able to mobilize support, either through traditional or electronic grass roots campaigning.

Limitations

Although we did capture a representative sample of political Facebook groups, we cannot rule out the possibility that certain groups were represented more than others. However, based on membership numbers alone, we believe we probably captured the most salient and important groups along with a nice array of others. Although we coded for what we deemed to be some of the most salient pieces of information on Facebook pages, we did not code other aspects of the page (Wall, Discussion Boards, and Posted Items) which might further explain the nature of candidate portrayals, and capture more nuanced themes in user discussion. Although the aspects we coded for represented the content that was under the control of the group administrators, these other aspects of the group page represent areas in which other group members can potentially engage in back-and-forth dialogue about the candidates and issues. However, the use of these aspects varies greatly, ranging from statements of support, to personal insults, to announcement of campaign events, and further analysis would be needed to determine the nature of this communication. Finally, given the current methodology, we can only speculate as to the motivations behind the user-generated content, and its potential effects on Facebook users and the political sphere in general.

Conclusions and Future Research

Prior research has found that formats of blogs, discussion boards, and campaign websites do indeed have features that aid in attracting supporters and have been suggested to have strong democratic potential (Papacharissi, 2004; Trammell et al., 2006). Although one study cannot definitively lead us to dismiss the democratic potential of Facebook, future research would need to focus on the content within Facebook groups where discussion that mirrors that of blogs and discussion boards are found. Facebook groups have a vast amount of content. By systematically analyzing more of that content, future research might be able to more concretely assess the whether these groups have the ability to increase participatory democracy or further exacerbate the polarizing of political viewpoints. Future research could also investigate the effects of, use of, and exposure to political Facebook groups in terms of voter attitudes, opinions, and participation.

ACKNOWLEDGMENT

The authors would like to thank Dr. Colleen Connolly-Ahern, Dr. David Perlmutter, and two anonymous reviewers for their insightful comments on earlier versions of this paper.

REFERENCES

Alexa: The Web Information Company. (2010). *Top 500 global sites.* Retrieved May 17, 2010, from http://www.alexa.com/topsites
Banning, S. A. (2006). Third person effects on political participation. *Journalism and Mass Communication Quarterly, 83,* 785–800.

Baumann, M. (2008). Barack Obama—master in social media marketing. *Max the Web*. Retrieved from http://maxtheweb.com/barack-obama-master-in-social-media-marketing

Bortree, D. S., & Seltzer, T. (2009). Dialogic strategies and outcomes: An analysis of environmental advocacy groups' Facebook profiles. *Public Relations Review, 35*, 317–319.

Boyd, D. M., & Ellison, N. B. (2007). Social network sites: Definition, history, and scholarship. *Journal of Computer-Mediated Communication, 13*(1), Article 11.

Brockett, A. A., & Baird, P. D. (2008). Media influence on the attitudes and knowledge of York adolescents towards Islam, Muslims, the Middle East and Arabs. *Journal of Arab and Muslim Media Research, 1*, 165–185.

Cary, M. K. (2009). President Barack Obama masters the new online media. *U.S. News & World Report*. Retrieved from http://www.usnews.com/blogs/mary-kate-cary/2009/01/26/president-barack-obama-masters-the-new-online-media.html

Creamer, M. (2007). Would you let these people friend you? *Advertising Age, 78*(32), 1–3.

Daft, R. L., & Lengel, R. H. (1984). Information richness: A new approach to managerial behavior and organizational design. In L. L. Cummings & B. M. Staw (Eds.), *Research in organizational behavior 6* (pp. 191–233). Homewood, IL: JAI Press.

Facebook Press Room. (2010). *Facebook statistics*. Retrieved May 15, 2010, from http://www.facebook.com/press/info.php?statistics

Ford, T. (1997). Effects of stereotypical television portrayals of African-Americans on person perception. *Social Psychology Quarterly, 60*, 266–278.

Golan, G., Banning, S., & Lundy, L. (2005, May). *Likelihood to vote, candidate choice and the third-person effect*. Paper delivered to the International Communication Association Annual Meeting, New York, NY.

Hayes, A. F., & Krippendorff, K. (2007). Answering the call for a standard reliability measure for coding data. *Communication Methods and Measures, 1*, 77–89.

Hill, H., Hickman, J., & McLendon, J. (2001). Cults and sects and doomsday groups, oh my: Media treatment of religion on the eve of the millennium. *Review of Religious Research, 43*(1), 24–38.

Inside Network. (2010). Facebook growth accelerates among older users in India. Retrieved September 27, 2010, from http://www.insidefacebook.com/2010/09/24/mexico-india-older-users/

Ivory, J., Williams, D., Martins, N., & Consalvo, M. (2009). Good clean fun? A content analysis of profanity in video games and its prevalence across game systems and ratings. *Cyberpsychology & Behavior, 12*, 1–4.

Iyengar, S., & Kinder, D. R. (1987). *News that matters: Television and American opinion*. Chicago: University of Chicago Press.

Johnston, A., & Kaid, L. (2002). Image ads and issue ads in U.S. presidential advertising: Using videostyle to explore stylistic differences in televised political ads from 1952 to 2000. *Journal of Communication, 52*, 281–300.

Jones, S., & Fox, S. (2009). Generational differences in online activities. *Pew Internet and American Life Project*. Retrieved May 1, 2010, from http://pewinternet.org/Infographics/Generational-differences-in-online-activities.aspx

Kaid, L., & Postelnicu, M. (2005). Political advertising in the 2004 election: Comparison of traditional television and internet messages. *American Behavioral Scientist, 49*, 265–278.

Kaye, B. K., & Sapolsky, B. S. (2004). Offensive language in primetime television: Four years after television age and content ratings. *Journal of Broadcasting & Electronic Media, 48*, 554–569.

Lee, M. M., Carpenter, B., & Meyers, L. S. (2007). Representations of older adults in television advertisements. *Journal of Aging Studies, 21*, 23–30.

Lee, T-T. (2005). The liberal media myth revisited: An examination of factors influencing perceptions of media bias. *Journal of Broadcasting and Electronic Media, 49*(1), 43–64.

Marks, G., & Miller, N. (1987). Ten years of research on the false-consensus effect: An empirical and theoretical review. *Psychological Bulletin, 102*(1), 72–90.

Mastro, D., & Greenberg, B. S. (2000). The portrayal of racial minorities on prime-time television. *Journal of Broadcasting and Electronic Media, 44*, 690–703.

McCombs, M. E. (2004). *Setting the agenda: The mass media and public opinion.* Cambridge, UK: Blackwell Polity Press..

Mckenzie-Mohr, D., & Zanna, M. P. (1990). Treating women as sexual objects: Look to the (gender schematic) male who has viewed pornography. *Personality and Social Psychology Bulletin, 16*, 296–308.

Mehta, C. R., & Patel, N. R. (1996). *SPSS exact tests.* Chicago: SPSS, Inc.

Miller, C. C. (2008). How Obama's internet campaign changed politics. *New York Times.* Retrieved March 17, 2010, from http://bits.blogs.nytimes.com/2008/11/07/how-obamas-internet-campaign-changed-politics/

Oliver, M. B. (1994). Portrayals of crime, race, and aggression in "reality-based" police shows: A content analysis. *Journal of Broadcasting & Electronic Media, 38*, 179–192.

O'Sullivan, P., & Flanagin, A. (2003). Reconceptualizing "flaming" and other problematic messages. *New Media & Society, 5*, 69–94.

Papacharissi, Z. (2004). Democracy online: Civility, politeness, and the democratic potential of online political discussion groups. *New Media & Society, 6*, 259–283.

Park, N., Kee, K. F., & Valenzuela, S. (2009). Being immersed in social networking environment: Facebook groups, uses and gratifications, and social outcomes. *Cyber Psychology & Behavior, 12*, 729–733.

Peterson, R. T., & Ross, D. T. (1997). A content analysis of the portrayal of mature individuals in television commercials. *Journal of Business Ethics, 16*, 425–433.

Quily, P. (2008). *Barack Obama vs. John McCain social media and search engine scorecard.* Retrieved May 1, 2010, from http://adultaddstrengths.com/2008/11/05/obama-vs-mccain-social-media/

Rawlinson, L. (2007). *Will the 2008 USA election be won on Facebook?* Retrieved May 1, 2010, from http://www.cnn.com/2007/TECH/05/01/election.facebook/

Rice, R. E. (1993). Media appropriateness: Using social presence theory to compare traditional and new organizational media. *Human Communication Research, 19*, 451–484.

Roy, A., & Harwood, J. (1997). Underrepresented, positively portrayed: Older adults in television commercials. *Journal of Applied Communication Research, 25*(1), 39–56.

Schufele, D. A. (1999). Framing as a theory of media effects. *Journal of Communication, 6*, 103–122.

Shah, D. V., Kwak, N., & Holbert, R. L. (2001). "Connecting" and "disconnecting" with civic life: Patterns of internet use and the production of social capital. *Political Communication, 18*, 141–162.

Short, J., Williams, E., & Christie, B. (1976). *The social psychology of telecommunications.* London: Wiley.

Smith, A. (2009). The Internet's role in campaign 2008. *Pew Internet & American Life Project.* Retrieved May 12, 2010, from http://pewinternet.org/Reports/2009/6-The-Internets-Role-in-Campaign-2008.aspx

Smith, J. (2008). 2008 statistics on American politics on Facebook. *Inside Facebook.* Retrieved May 12, 2010, from http://www.insidefacebook.com/2008/01/02/2008-statistics-on-american-politics-on-facebook

Stern, S. R., & Mastro, D. E. (2004). Gender portrayals across the lifespan: A content analytic look at broadcast commercials. *Mass Communication and Society, 7*, 215–236.

Stout, D. A., & Buddenbaum, J. M. (2003). Media, religion, and "framing." *Journal of Media and Religion, 2*(1), 1–3.

Sunstein, C. (2001). *Republic.com*. Princeton, NJ: Princeton University Press.

Sunstein, C. (2007). *Republic.com 2.0*. Princeton, NJ: Princeton University Press.

Sweetser, K., & Lariscy, R. (2008). Candidates make good friends: An analysis candidates' uses of Facebook. *International Journal of Strategic Communication, 2,* 175–208.

Tanis, M., & Postmes, T. (2003). Social cues and impression formation in CMC. *Journal of Communication, 53,* 676–693.

Trammell, K., Williams, A., Postelnicu, M., & Landreville, K. (2006). Evolution of online campaigning: Increasing interactivity in candidate websites and blogs through text and technical features. *Mass Communication & Society, 9*(1), 21–44.

Vargas, J. A. (2007). Young voters find voice of Facebook. *Washington Post*. Retrieved April 22, 2009, from http://www.washingtonpost.com/wp-dyn/content/article/2007/02/16/AR2007021602084.html

Vestweber, D. (1992). Prime-time plots: A content analysis of changes in gender representation. *Journal of Broadcasting & Electronic Media, 36*(1), 25–50.

Vitak, J., Smock, A., Zube, P., Carr, C., Ellison, N., & Lampe, C. (2009, May). *"Poking" people to participate: Facebook and political participation in the 2008 election*. Paper presented at the 2009 Annual Meeting of the International Communication Association, Chicago, IL.

Walther, J. B. (1992). Interpersonal effects in computer-mediated interaction: A relational perspective. *Communication Research, 19,* 52–90.

Walther, J. B. (1993). Impression development in computer-mediated interaction. *Western Journal of Communication, 57,* 473–501.

Walther, J. B. (1996). Computer-mediated communication: Impersonal, interpersonal, and hyperpersonal interaction. *Communication Research, 23,* 3–43.

Walther, J. B., Anderson, J., & Park, D. (1994). Interpersonal effects in computer-mediated communication: A meta-analysis of social and anti-social communication. *Communication Research, 21,* 460–487.

Westling, M. (2007). Expanding the public sphere: The impact of Facebook on political communication. *The New Vernacular*. Retrieved May 16, 2008, from http://www.thenewvernacular.com/projects/facebook_and_political_communication.pdf

Williams, C., & Gulati, G. (2007). *Social networks in political campaigns: Facebook and the 2006 midterm elections*. Paper presented at the 2007 Annual Meeting of the American Political Science Association, Chicago, IL.

Yao, Q. (2007). China's official framing of religion and its influence on young Chinese students: A partial testing of the process model of framing in a special media environment. *Asian Journal of Communication, 17,* 416–432.

The Writing on the Wall: A Content Analysis of College Students' Facebook Groups for the 2008 Presidential Election

Juliana Fernandes
School of Journalism and Mass Communication
Florida International University

Magda Giurcanu
Department of Political Science
University of Florida

Kevin W. Bowers and Jeffrey C. Neely
College of Journalism and Communications
University of Florida

This study looks at student Facebook groups supporting the 2008 presidential candidates, John McCain and Barack Obama, from largest land-grant universities in seven battleground states. The findings of a content analysis of wall posts show that students are using Facebook to facilitate dialog and civic political involvement. In opposition to pro-McCain groups, pro-Obama groups have wider time frame coverage and demonstrate substantively higher site activity. Political discussions related to the political civic process, policy issues, campaign information, candidate issues, and acquisition of campaign products dominate across groups and election seasons. An examination of the content of wall posts based on the four categories of the Michigan Model of voting behavior (partisanship, group affiliation, candidate image, and political/campaign issues) reveals that in the primary season, pro-Obama groups focus mostly on short-term topics (candidate image and campaign issues), whereas pro-McCain groups focus mostly on long-term topics (partisanship and group affiliation). The overall findings of this study suggest that youth online communities actively follow campaigns and post comments that foster the political dialog and civic engagement.

In recent years, scholars started to focus their attention on understanding the role of online political communication (Ancu & Cozma, 2009; Endres & Warnick, 2004; Postelnicu & Cozma, 2007a, 2007b; Shah et al., 2007; Stromer-Galley & Foot, 2002; Sweetser & Lariscy, 2008; Trammell, 2007; Wells & Dudash, 2007). In a political campaign environment, the Internet proved to be an excellent medium for dissemination of information, mobilization, social interaction, and even entertainment (Ancu & Cozma, 2009; Stromer-Galley & Foot, 2002). Historically used for the first time in a campaign context in 1996, the Internet played a major role in the 2004 presidential election when campaigns made a strategic move and began writing blogs (Trammell, 2007). The Internet played a similar role in the 2006 midterm Congressional elections when candidates for U.S. Senate and House of Representatives were invited by Facebook, a student-originated site used primarily by a younger-than-29 age demographic, to participate and host profiles like other users (Sweetser & Lariscy, 2008). At least one third of the candidates running for U.S. Senate seats responded to the invitation and posted their profiles on Facebook (Williams & Gulati, 2007). Moreover, in the 2008 presidential election, all Democratic and Republican candidates established Facebook and MySpace profiles, and hundreds of thousands of social network sites (SNSs) users added them as "friends" (Ancu & Cozma, 2009).

The use of the Internet to develop election-oriented Web sites (e.g., candidate/campaign Web sites and Facebook and MySpace profiles) is praised in the literature on political communication as the "greatest dialogic move" (Sweetser & Lariscy, 2008, p. 176) because it allows for open and active political dialog between candidates or representatives of the campaign and voters or among constituents themselves. However, despite this possibility for two-way communication and active human interaction between politicians and voters, previous studies document that this potential is not being actualized (Stromer-Galley & Foot, 2002). From the constituents' perspective, such Web sites are appreciated for their depth of political information and accessibility as opposed to other sources of political information (e.g., debates, news on television, or candidate ads). From the candidates' perspective, the exchange of political ideas in a conversational style is burdensome (Endres & Warnick, 2004) because it involves the risk of losing control over what is said (Postelnicu & Cozma, 2007a; Stromer-Galley, 2000). As a result, only a few candidates actually engage in dialogic communication with their constituents on Facebook (Sweetser & Lariscy, 2008). Moreover, citizens themselves do not demand greater exchanges of policy opinions from politicians (Stromer-Galley & Foot, 2002), and comments posted on candidates' walls are frequently personal in content, whereas comments addressed to other voters are richer in political content (Postelnicu & Cozma, 2007b).

The purpose of this study is to analyze how one such SNS, Facebook, facilitated political dialog and civic engagement in the context of the 2008 presidential election. In contrast to other studies that focused on SNSs and candidate-to-voter interactions, this research builds on the empirical evidence of wall post discussions among voters themselves. In a nutshell, it looks for political dialog in places where, based on previous research, it is more likely to be found, in voter-to-voter online interactions. Such SNSs are, however, mostly popular among young people, a demographic that is not necessarily actively involved in politics. Youth voters have been underrepresented since 1976 when 18- to 21-year-olds were given the right to vote (Iyengar & Jackman, 2004), and in general, voter turnout among this age group has constantly declined (Levine & Lopez, 2002). Despite the documented apathy among youth, the 2008 presidential election registered a big surge in voters ages 18 to 29 (CIRCLE, 2008). In addition, the youth supported Barack Obama, regardless of their political affiliation, crossing both partisan and racial lines (CIRCLE, 2008). Getting insights into youth conversations on social network Web sites for political purposes certainly deserves attention, especially in the context of both a recent turnout surge and a particular candidate's overwhelming popularity.

This study investigates wall post content of nine college student Facebook groups in seven battleground states, supporting either one of the Democratic and Republican candidates for U.S. president—Barack Obama and John McCain. The research questions investigate: How are students using this forum for political civic involvement? Do voter-to-voter conversations suggest that SNSs are *mainly* sources for social interaction with other like-minded supporters as previous research supports (Ancu & Cozma, 2009), or are the SNSs used to facilitate political dialog and civic involvement? If political discussions dominate, are they reflecting more the long-term influences of party and group allegiances, or are discussions mostly concerned with short-term aspects of political behavior such as issues and candidates' images? Are comments mostly positive toward the candidate they support, as previous studies attest in candidate-to-voter interactions (Postelnicu & Cozma, 2007b; Sweetser & Lariscy, 2008) or are they mostly negative when referring to either the supported candidate or the opponent?

THEORETICAL BACKGROUND

SNSs offer an entirely new way for people to be involved with the political process, and their popularity among youth suggests that SNSs may be a powerful tool for bringing young voters back into the political process. Such participatory media provide voters, and youth in particular, with an opportunity to be directly involved in the political process without leaving their homes or offices (Stromer-Galley & Foot, 2002). SNSs allow for discussions, debates, and grassroot mobilizations for issues that young voters care about (Rheingold, 2008), encouraging participatory behaviors (Shah et al., 2007). Through online conversations, youth can speak on their own behalf about their unique concerns and positions regarding policies and can organize themselves for defending such positions. Because discussions with others and the Internet are the main sources youth utilize to gain political knowledge (Wells & Dudash, 2007), SNSs seem to be the optimal environment for promoting youth political involvement.

What type of conversations do youth display on Facebook? Building on research that documents political conversations among voters themselves rather than between voters and politicians (Ancu & Cozma, 2009), the researchers hypothesized that Facebook groups would display voter-to-voter conversations that are mainly political in nature, rather than simply reflecting social interaction or entertainment needs. In addition, the researchers hypothesized that Barack Obama's supporting groups would show higher site activity and membership than John McCain's groups. Besides young voters' overwhelming support for Barack Obama reported by surveys (Kanel & Quinley, 2008; Keeter, Horowitz, & Tyson, 2008), news reports suggested that Barack Obama was far more effective than his opponent in tapping into the power of

SNSs (Carr, 2008). Barack Obama's integration of SNSs into his campaign is said to have given his supporters a sense of involvement and gave his campaign organizers a direct line of contact with the constituents ("McCain vs. Obama," 2008). Thus, the first two hypotheses are as follows:

H1: Facebook groups supporting Barack Obama will show a higher level of site activity and membership than Facebook groups supporting John McCain.
H2: Content on Facebook groups supporting one of the two major candidates of the 2008 U.S. presidential election will focus more on political discussions than on social interaction.

If these conversations are primarily political in content, what aspects of the voting behavior model, also known as the Michigan Model, are dominant? Do topics reflect more long-term allegiances of partisanship and primary group associations, or are topics more concerned with short-term influences of policy issues and candidates' images? The Michigan Model explains political behavior during elections and has been extensively used in classifying political communication (Joslyn, 1980; Kaid, McKinney, & Tedesco, 2000). Using data from political surveys conducted from 1948 through 1958, *The American Voter*, the breakthrough work that introduced the Michigan Model, established four categories of factors that influence the public's attitude toward politics and thus influence its decisions when going to the polls (Campbell, Converse, Miller, & Stokes, 1964).

The most important category of the Michigan Model and the starting point of Campbell et al.'s (1964) analysis is partisanship. Partisan orientation and a sense of party identification are recognized as having an enduring effect on the public's attitude toward politics, and partisanship loyalty is provided as a plausible explanation for why American politics is dominated by only two parties. However, the stability of a person's perceptions of political events and even his partisan allegiance expressed at the polls depends also on the enduring social groupings that divide the electorate. That is, group opinion serves as a reference point and reinforces the individual's perception of what his political stance should be based on irrespective of party affiliation. Campbell and associates (1964) suggested that primary group associations, such as family, work, or even friendship, with the high degree of homogeneity built into them, can surpass and contradict partisan attitudes. However, due to the decrease in the people in the electorate who identify themselves as Democrats or Republicans and the increase in the number of

Independents registered in the 1970s, some scholars have promoted the "partisan decline thesis" (Bartels, 2000) and asserted that partisanship and group memberships are not the sole influences on how voters practice politics.

Short-term aspects of politics, such as candidate image and policy issues, have become critical components in explaining political attitudes and behavior (Boyd, 1972; Joslyn, 1980). As a result, the impact of party allegiance expressed at the polls is much more variable than previously admitted. A candidate's appeal as a person has shown to play a major role in voters reaching a final decision. Specifically, aspects of a candidate's personal life, such as record of leadership, reputation, personal integrity, and charisma, can easily disturb long-term commitments. Finally, even though one of the greatest limitations for civic participation is a general lack of public awareness of major social and economic problems, issues and specific policy matters do play an important role in explaining voting behavior. Thus, knowledge of party positions on specific policy issues will influence voting behavior, even though such concerns apply only to a minority of the population (Campbell et al., 1964). In sum, four categories affect political behavior: two concerned with long-term loyalties, partisan or primary groupings, and two concerned with short-term influences, candidate image and policy issues.

Considering this, which influences of the Michigan Model led to the election of Barack Obama in 2008? Are the identified influences for the entire population also applicable to young voters? In a retrospective of the 2008 campaign, Campbell (2008) suggested that the decisive factor in Obama's victory was the mid-September Wall Street meltdown crisis in financial institutions. In many respects, the 2008 presidential election was exceptional (Campbell, 2008): a strong negative reaction against an incumbent president, an unpopular war, and a sluggish economy were announcing 2008 to be a Democratic year. However, the pre-election conditions were offset by a moderate conservative Republican candidate preferred by a center-right nation in opposition to a northern-liberal Democratic candidate, only to be overturned again by a Wall Street financial crisis. Partisan parity and ideological polarization, an open seat election, in addition to a protracted battle for the nomination process in the Democratic camp, transformed the 2008 election in a very tight race, such that in early September 2008 McCain was taking the lead in Gallup polls. By October 6, 2008, however, after the financial collapse, the battle was decided in favor of the Democratic candidate that promoted "change" (Campbell, 2008, pp. 15–16).

Although Campbell (2008) acknowledged the relevance of long-term influences such as partisanship and underscored as decisive short-term factors such as candidates' positions and economic issues, Martinez (2009), in a study of Floridians' electoral behavior in the 2008 election, posited that the decisive factors in the 2008 presidential election for Florida were partisanship and a strong reaction against the incumbent Bush administration.

Thus, yet another question is raised: Which factors of the aforementioned possible explanations are relevant for youth? The researchers proposed that the content analysis of youth conversations in Facebook groups involved in the 2008 presidential campaign would shed light on this question. Previous research on political attitudes and campaigns has documented that people, in general, want substantive information about a candidate's position on issues, followed by information on his experience, character, and intelligence (Lipsitz, Trost, Grossmann, & Sides, 2005). However, in a study on MySpace comments addressed to 2006 congressional candidates, Postelnicu and Cozma (2007b) found that most of the conversation focused on campaign events and candidates' images, whereas policy issues were rarely addressed. In addition to the short-term focus during the campaigns, age tends to create fixed attitudes such that issue discussions are more useful for younger voters because it may enhance their understanding of the political process and acquisition of political knowledge (Lipsitz et al., 2005). Therefore, considering these previous findings, the researchers hypothesized the following:

H3: Facebook groups' discussion will focus mostly on the short-term influences of candidate image and policy issues as identified by traditional voting behavior models, rather than on long-term influences of party identification and group affiliation.

The last question addressed in this study refers to the overall tone of the conversation in the Facebook groups. Previous studies on voter-to-candidate conversations on SNSs found that comments are generally, positive in tone, polite, highly civil, and supportive of candidates (Ancu & Cozma, 2009; Postelnicu & Cozma, 2007b; Sweetser & Lariscy, 2008). Given the tight race and the higher stakes of the presidential election compared to previous studies that researched online content for midterm congressional elections, the researchers expected the conversations to be mostly positive in content, but negative aspects are not necessarily excluded. Thus, the final hypotheses are as follows:

H4: Candidate mentions on Facebook groups will demonstrate praise for the group's candidate rather than criticism for the respective candidate or the opposing candidate.

H4a: The overall tone of the wall posts on these Facebook groups will be positive as the focus will be in supporting the group's candidate rather than negative.

METHOD

The researchers were looking to tap into youth political conversation in an online environment. Although young voters are comfortable using SNSs, they might not be as interested in displaying political conversations. Because previous research on political behavior attests that political interest increases with education, higher stakes, and uncertainty of the political outcome (Campbell, 1960; Tufte, 1975), the researchers optimized the sample by selecting Facebook groups with high values on two of the variables mentioned: education and uncertainty of the final outcome. A presidential election is already a high-stakes election as opposed to local or midterm congressional elections. Thus, this study used content analysis to examine student Facebook groups for the two main presidential candidates, John McCain and Barack Obama, at land-grant universities in seven swing states during the 2008 presidential campaign. The analysis was limited to the front pages and wall posts of the selected universities and candidates. The Facebook groups selected in gathering the sample came from universities in states considered "swing" states by two of three major sources of election coverage: CNN, the *New York Times*, and the *Washington Post*. Each of these news organizations had a list of swing states, which was gathered from the election sections of their Web sites one week before the election. The final list of swing states listed by at least two of these three sources were Colorado, Florida, Indiana, Missouri, Nevada, North Carolina, and Ohio ("CNN Electoral Map Calculator", 2008; "The Electoral Map", 2008; "2008 Political Landscape Map", 2008). Searches of Facebook groups were then made using the state name, candidate name, and various forms of the largest land-grant university names as search terms. These universities were Colorado State University; University of Florida; Purdue University; University of Missouri; University of Nevada, Reno; North Carolina State University; and The Ohio State University. Facebook groups for John McCain were found at only three of the seven universities, and for Barack Obama at six of the seven universities. In cases where multiple student Facebook groups existed in support for the same candidate, the group with the largest membership was selected. The front page of each Facebook group in the sample was downloaded and archived one week before the election and resulted in nine Facebook groups between both presidential candidates.

The unit of analysis for this project was an individual wall post. The wall posts for each group were downloaded and archived after the election. All wall posts from the beginning of the Facebook group through November 4, 2008, were used for the analysis. This resulted in 562 wall posts (pro-Obama posts, $n = 511$; pro-McCain posts, $n = 51$) from the nine Facebook groups selected.

Content Categories

To group the wall posts, each post was coded for basic demographics of the commenter (gender, student affiliation), group-related information (the university the group represented, the candidate the group supported), and date. To determine the presence of political conversations, a similar set of content categories was created based on studies that addressed online media and youth conversation during campaigns on blogs (Trammell, 2007) and social media research (Postelnicu & Cozma, 2007b; Sweetser & Lariscy, 2008). The posts were then analyzed for the presence of a specified list of topics, which included political civic process (voter registration, volunteering, get out the vote, political meeting, rally, watch a debate/speech), policy discussions, horse race coverage, selling products/acquisition of campaign products, Web link, social related activities (social event, nonpolitical meeting), relationship building/interpersonal support, request to join another group, emotional expressions (positive emotional expression toward the candidates the group supports or negative emotional expression toward the candidates the group supports), and "other."

Because the "other" category became dominant in our initial coding (i.e., 20% of the wall posts fitted in the other category), a qualitative analysis was performed to further investigate which topics were relevant in the wall posts. As a result of this analysis, four subcategories of topics were included: (a) candidate issues: topics related to the candidate supported by the group and his campaign, discussions about candidate's preferences and appearances in the area; (b) negative statements about the opponents: opponents could be identified as Republicans, Hillary Clinton, John McCain and his supporters, Barack Obama and his supporters; (c) organizational/administrative activities for the group: inquiries about group's meetings, Web design, future activities, group size, and notes praising the group members for their work; and (d) other. In addition, because some of the initial categories had only a minimal coverage (e.g., negative statements about the candidate the group supports, relationship building/interpersonal support, and request to join another group), the researchers decided to collapse some of these categories as follows: social related topics and relationship building became one category, labeled as social topics; negative emotional expressions for opponents and for supported candidates became one category, labeled as negative expressions; and group organizational activities and request to join another group became also one category, labeled as group organizational activities.

To tap into the political content defined in terms of the Michigan Model, the four categories established by this model were used. These four categories were then divided into two subgroups. The first subgroup encompasses long-term influences, such as party affiliation (i.e., when the wall post clearly stated the political party to which the poster belongs to) and group preferences/affiliation (i.e., when the wall post mentioned the poster's preference for a group (e.g., religious, labor unions, students, etc.) that is not the Facebook group). The following examples help illustrate each of these categories:

"Commenter A[1] wrote on January 7, 2008: Congratulations to Jessica on becoming a Obama Delegate to the Democratic National Convention in August!" (example of party affiliation)

"Commenter B wrote on July 5, 2007: "...We are proud to announce that Senator Barack Obama will be in attendance at the NAACP convention, in Detroit, on July 12, 2007! During the days leading up to his arrival we will need volunteers at the convention to bring enthusiasm!" (example of group preferences/affiliation)

The second subgroup encompasses short-term influences, such as campaign/political issues (i.e., when the wall post mentioned campaign issues and/or political issues) and candidate image (i.e., when the wall post discussed candidate image, such as physical characteristics, personality characteristics, experience, biographic information, qualifications). The following examples illustrate the short-term influences:

"Commenter C wrote on October 17, 2008:...I think high school students and college students should ask themselves and each other: How will we find a job after we finish HS or college if Obama is president? His tax plan will raise taxes on companies from 35% to 39%, when America has the highest taxes on companies in the world already." (example of campaign/political issues)

"Commenter D wrote on February 12, 2008: Obama wrote about his drug use in 1995. It's not really new news. I was surprised to see it in the Alligator. Big deal though. Show me a person that has never made a mistake and I'll show you a liar." (example of candidate image)

Finally, the tone of each wall post was considered in terms of positive, negative, equal mix of positive and negative, or neutral. Comments about

---

[1]Commenters' names were changed to letters (e.g., Commenter A, B, etc.) to preserve their anonymity.

presidential or vice-presidential candidates, John McCain, Sarah Palin, and Barack Obama (Joe Biden was never mentioned) were recorded and classified in terms of personal criticism, policy criticism, or positive statement.

Coding Process

The authors, who served as the coders, co-coded 60 random wall posts of the 562 total wall posts for an average percentage agreement of 94.9% and a range of agreement from 69.4% to 100%. Of all categories included in the analysis, only two of them had a percentage of agreement below 80%.[2] Based on its use on similar studies, Scott's Pi was used to determine reliability accounting for chance agreement and produced a reliability coefficient of 0.74 across all categories. Intercoder reliability was calculated using the software ReCal (Freelon, 2008). Because the level of agreement was considered satisfactory, the coders divided the entire sample for coding. The authors utilized a codebook that contained a detailed explanation of all content categories previously mentioned.

Sample Characteristics

Nine Facebook groups (pro-Obama, $n = 6$; pro-McCain, $n = 3$) were analyzed in this study. Among all nine groups, the University of Florida groups had the largest membership for both candidates. The "UF Students for Obama (Official Chapter)" had 1,861 members, and the "Gators for McCain" had 563 members. The most active groups in terms of number of wall posts were the pro-Obama groups at the University of Florida, followed by The Ohio State University, and North Carolina State University, whereas the pro-McCain groups were mainly represented by students at the University of Florida (see Table 1).

The demographics of the sample in the pro-Obama groups consisted of 48% male posters and 44% female posters. For pro-McCain groups, male posters represented 59% of the sample, while female posters covered 35% of the sample.

The researchers noticed that pro-Obama groups had a wider time frame than pro-McCain groups, with four out of five groups starting their activity in 2007 when the official primary season had not begun yet. Pro-McCain groups, on the other hand, posted their first comments only in February 2008. Considering the protracted intraparty battle for the Democratic nomination, we speculate that the wider time frame for pro-Obama groups might

---

[2]Coders indicated the dominant topic (see Table 2 for a list of topics) for each wall post and the percentage of agreement for this category was 69.4%. Overall tone of the wall post had a 73.8% percentage of agreement.

TABLE 1
Sample Characteristics

Candidate supported	University name	No. of wall posts	No. of members	Time frame
Barack Obama				
	University of Florida	277	1861	Aug 6, 2007 – Nov 13, 2008
	Ohio State University	99	561	July 5, 2007 – Nov 6, 2008
	North Carolina State University	79	428	July 9, 2008 – Nov 5, 2008
	Purdue University	31	462	Feb 6, 2008 – Nov 6, 2008
	University of Missouri	30	592	Aug 30, 2007 – Nov 18, 2008
	Colorado State University	23	166	Oct 6, 2007 – Oct 23, 2008
	Total	539	4070	
John McCain				
	University of Florida	41	563	Feb 8, 2008 – Nov 3, 2008
	University of Nevada, Reno	5	167	June 6, 2008 – Oct 3, 2008
	Ohio State University	5	64	Oct 5, 2008 – Oct 26, 2008
	Total	51	794	

be related to a more disputed campaign environment. At the time when first pro-Obama wall posts appear, Hillary Clinton was generally perceived in the popular press as the preferred candidate (Balz & Johnson, 2009). To have a deeper perspective on political comments in a campaign environment, the researchers decided to divide the sample based on the two election seasons: (a) intraparty competition during the primary season (covering all wall posts before August 31, 2008) and (b) interparty competition during the general season (September 1, 2008, to November 4, 2008). Each hypothesis proposed in this study investigates differences between the two election seasons, in addition to trends for the entire election.

RESULTS

The first hypothesis predicted that pro-Obama groups would be more active than the pro-McCain groups. The data easily confirm this hypothesis, as 91% of wall posts in the overall sample belong to the pro-Obama groups, whereas only 9% of wall posts represent the pro-McCain groups. A two-sample test of a proportion shows that the two groups are different in terms of wall post activity ($z = 27.44$, $p = .000$), with the qualification that pro-Obama groups are more active than the pro-McCain groups ($p < .05$, for one-sided hypothesis). A distribution of wall post activity across the two election seasons for each group shows that more than half of all pro-Obama comments were posted during the primary season and only 38% during the general election season. The distribution of wall posts for McCain groups is reversed: 74% of all pro-McCain comments are posted during the general season. The researchers speculate that higher site activity for pro-Obama groups during the primary season was related to the tight intraparty race between Barack Obama and Hillary Clinton.

The second hypothesis suggested that content on Facebook groups supporting one of the major candidates of the 2008 U.S. presidential election would focus more on political civic participation than on social interaction. A summary of topics across all wall posts shows that these groups covered a wide array of categories, from political topics to social interactions, Web link, group organizational activities, and emotional expressions (see Table 2, Dominant topics). Political topics related to the political civic process, policy discussions, candidate issues, horse race coverage, and acquisition of campaign products represent more than half of wall posts for the overall election and for each season. At the same time, social-related activities reflect no more than 5% of wall posts, for the entire election coverage and for each election season. This finding suggests that when the online youth communities are formed with the goal of supporting a political candidate, social activities are relegated and the focus on the political process itself becomes more important. In addition, the distribution of dominant topics across the two election seasons is different, $\chi^2(10) = 32.46$, $p = .000$, such that group organizational activities decrease from 13.44% during the primary season to 4.87% in the general season. A similar decrease is noted for positive emotional expressions, from 9.69% to 4.87%, whereas the negative emotional expressions increase, from 2.5% to 6.19%. To understand these dynamics within each group, the researchers tabulated the percentage of dominant topic for each group during each season (see Table 3, Dominant topics). Overall, the statistical analyses show that Obama and McCain groups differ in terms of dominant topic distributions for each of the two seasons. However, despite significant statistical results, $\chi^2(6) = 12.54$, $p = .051$, and $\chi^2(6) = 6.19$, $p = .002$, due to the small sample size of pro-McCain groups, only the result for the general election season is reliable. The researchers noticed some major changes for McCain groups: During the primary season, these groups display 30.77% of political topics, 23.08% of social topics, 15.38% of positive emotional expressions, and 0% negative emotional expressions. During the general season, on the other hand, the political topics double, social topics disappear, positive emotional expressions decrease to 5%, and negative emotional expressions increase to 13.16%. The researchers considered that the increase in negativity for McCain groups was related to the tight race and to the negative prospects for McCain after mid-September. According to Campbell

TABLE 2
Analyses of Differences Between Election Seasons

	Overall election	Primary election season	General election season
Dominant topics[a] (%)			
Political topics			
Political civic process	39.56	36.88	43.36
Policy issues	4.03	4.69	3.10
Candidate issues	3.48	3.44	3.54
Horse race	5.13	6.56	3.10
Acquisition of campaign products	4.95	4.06	6.19
Social related topics			
Social interactions & relationship building	4.58	5.00	3.98
Web link	13.74	10.31	18.58
Group organizational activities	9.89	13.44	4.87
Emotional expressions			
Positive	7.69	9.69	4.87
Negative	4.03	2.50	6.19
Other	2.93	3.44	2.21
Michigan Model[b] (%)			
Long term			
Party	9.47	6.80	13.54
Group	28.81	23.81	36.46
Short term			
Candidate	23.05	24.49	20.83
Campaign/Political issues	38.68	44.90	29.17
Tone[c] (%)			
Positive	42.70	47.11	36.48
Negative	8.72	6.69	11.59
Equal mix	7.65	8.81	6.01
Neutral	40.93	37.39	45.92

Note. Statistical tests for differences between the two seasons (all expected counts > 5). [a]$\chi^2(10) = 32.46$, $p = .000$, *Cramér's* $V = 0.24$. [b]$\chi^2(3) = 10.06$, $p = .018$, *Cramér's* $V = 0.20$. [c]$\chi^2(3) = 11.20$, $p = .011$, *Cramér's* $V = 0.14$.

(2008), the race between Obama and McCain was very tight during the general season up to the financial crisis meltdown, such that by October 6, the battle was already decided in Obama's favor. In addition, The Ohio State University McCain group forms on October 5 and displays mainly negative comments toward Obama, his supporters, and his campaign. It is likely that the late formation of this group might have been triggered by the possible Obama win and the willingness of McCain supporters to try to undermine the opponent, thus increasing the amount of negative comments in the wall posts. In sum, considering the higher site activity for Obama groups during the primary season and the dominance of political topics across wall

TABLE 3
Analyses of Differences Between Groups by Election Seasons

	Primary election season		General election season	
	Obama groups	McCain groups	Obama groups	McCain groups
Dominant topics[a] (%)				
Political civic process	56.68	30.77	59.04	60.53
Social activities	4.23	23.08	4.79	0.00
Web link	10.10	15.38	19.68	13.16
Group organizational activities	13.68	7.69	4.79	5.26
Emotional expressions				
Positive	9.45	15.38	4.79	5.26
Negative	2.61	0.00	4.79	13.16
Other	3.26	7.69	2.13	2.63
Michigan Model[b] (%)				
Long term				
Party	5.67	33.33	9.86	24.00
Group	22.70	50.00	39.44	28.00
Short term				
Candidate	24.82	16.67	22.54	16.00
Campaign	46.81	0.00	28.17	32.00
Tone[c] (%)				
Positive	46.20	69.23	38.97	23.68
Negative	6.65	7.69	8.72	26.32
Equal mix	8.86	7.69	6.67	2.63
Neutral	38.29	16.38	45.64	47.37

Note. Statistics for differences among groups in the primary season: [a]$\chi^2(6) = 12.54$, $p = .051$, Cramér's $V = 0.19$ (expected counts < 5). [b]$\chi^2(3) = 11.24$, $p = .010$, Cramér's $V = 0.28$ (expected counts < 5). [c]$\chi^2(3) = 3.20$, $p = .36$, Cramér's $V = .09$ (expected counts > 5). Statistics for differences among groups in the general season: [a]$\chi^2(6) = 6.19$, $p = .002$, Cramér's $V = .16$ (expected counts > 5). [b]$\chi^2(6) = 3.87$, $p = .28$, Cramér's $V = 0.20$ (expected counts < 5). [c]$\chi^2(3) = 11.41$, $p = .01$, Cramér's $V = .22$ (expected counts > 5).

comments, we posit that the quantitative and qualitative analyses show that tight races with high stakes, such as presidential elections, spur youth political involvement.

The third hypothesis predicted that the political discussions found in the wall posts would focus on short-term influences such as candidate image and political/campaign issues rather than on long-term influences such as party identification and group affiliation. As Table 2 (Michigan Model) shows, short-term topics cover more than 60% of political topics, most of them referring to campaign political issues (38.68%). If these results are disaggregated based on election seasons, we see that political topic distributions are statistically different, $\chi^2(3) = 10.06$, $p = .018$, such that in the primary campaign political issues dominate, whereas in the general season group related political topics dominate. To understand why in the general season there is an equal distribution of short- and long-term topics, the researchers present the Michigan Model topics across groups and seasons (see Table 3, Michigan Model). During the primary season, the pro-Obama groups are concerned mostly with the short-term influences of campaign issues (47%) and candidate image (25%), whereas the pro-McCain groups focus on the opposite, group affiliation (50%) and party (33%) discussions. During the general election season, short- and long-term political topics become somewhat evenly distributed among the two groups. Due to the small sample size for McCain groups, the statistical results presented in Table 3 are not reliable. However, two findings should be noticed: the competitive intraparty battle for the Democrats in the primary season tilted the discussions toward short-term topics, especially campaign-related issues. Second, for both seasons, young pro-Obama students, presumably Democrats, displayed significant lower percentages for partisanship as opposed to young Republicans (5.67 and 9.86 vs. 33.33 and 24.00). This finding, although not statistically significant, corroborates previous research that suggests that the pull of partisanship on voter choice is stronger for Republicans than for Democrats (Martinez, 2009).

The fourth hypothesis proposed that mentions of the candidates, across all student Facebook groups examined, would mostly praise the candidate the groups supported rather than criticize (personal or policy criticism) the respective candidate or opposing candidates. As Table 4 shows, among pro-Obama groups, when Barack Obama is mentioned, less than 1% of the wall posts personally criticize him, 1% of the time his policies are criticized, and 57% of the mentions are positive. Among the pro-McCain groups,

TABLE 4
Candidates Mentioned in Wall Posts (%)

	Personal criticism	Policy criticism	Positive mention
Barack Obama			
Mentioned in Obama groups	0.83[a]	1.24	56.61
Mentioned in McCain groups	23.07	46.15	0.00
John McCain			
Mentioned in Obama groups	24.14	17.24	3.45
Mentioned in McCain groups	0.00	0.00	71.43
Sarah Palin			
Mentioned in Obama groups	50.00	0.00	7.14
Mentioned in McCain groups	11.11	0.00	77.78

[a]Percentage of wall posts that mention Obama and personally criticize him among Obama groups.

McCain is praised on 71% of the wall posts, whereas Palin was positively mentioned on 78% of the pro-McCain wall posts. These high percentages confirm the initial hypothesis that support groups would mostly focus on praising the respective candidate rather than criticizing the group's candidate or the opponents. However, wall post content engages in personal and policy criticisms for the opponents. Obama is personally criticized on 23% of all wall posts of pro-McCain groups and criticized for policies on 46% of wall posts. McCain is personally criticized on 24% of posts, and his policies are criticized on 17% of the wall posts in pro-Obama groups. Finally, Palin is personally criticized on both pro-Obama and pro-McCain wall posts. Therefore, H4 is confirmed. Within supporting groups, wall post content is mostly concerned with praising the supported candidates. At the same time, a considerable percentage of wall posts criticize the opponents, perhaps in an effort to reinforce allegiance from still unconvinced supporters.

The final hypothesis predicted that the overall tone of the wall posts on these Facebook groups would be mostly positive. As Table 2 (Tone) shows, most wall posts have a positive tone (42.7% for the entire election, 47% in the primary and somewhat less during the general season, 36.48%). In the general season, negativity increases and this finding has been already noted when discussing the negative emotional expressions. The increase in negativity is driven by The Ohio State University pro-McCain group, formed a month before Election Day. Indeed, tone wall topics tabulated by support groups and election seasons in Table 3 (Tone) show that tone distributions among pro-Obama and pro-McCain groups are statistically different for the general season, mainly because of the increase in negativity among pro-McCain comments, $\chi^2(3) = 11.41$, $p = .01$.

DISCUSSION

This study investigated how SNSs, such as Facebook, facilitate political dialog and civic engagement among youth voter-to-voter online interactions. A content analysis of nine student Facebook groups from seven universities located in swing states revealed that such SNSs have a positive impact on youth political involvement. Topics related to the political civic process dominated across comments for both candidates in the primary and general election seasons. This evidence is in agreement with previous research (Ancu & Cozma, 2009; Rheingold, 2008; Shah et al., 2007; Stromer-Galley & Foot, 2002) that looked at how SNSs provide a space for voters, particularly young voters, to participate in the political process. In addition, this finding complements the literature on SNS as it uniquely reveals that the political discussion is dominant among voter-to-voter interactions. Indeed, young voters spend time online to network with other like-minded people (Postelnicu & Cozma, 2007b) but use the medium to transmit pertinent information related to candidates' campaign, issues, and appearances in the area. By way of contrast, students rarely used the Facebook groups examined in this study for purely social purposes. Moreover, online conversations blend with offline participatory activities because comments on wall posts often refer to group organizational activities, meetings, watching debates, and active involvement in campaigns by tabling, or acquiring campaign products (e.g., T-shirts, pins, posters). One could argue, therefore, that the online community becomes a real community outside the SNS medium.

In addition to the increase in human interaction on the wall and off the wall, Facebook is a popular venue for students to promote other online resources, such as Web links, which confirms the media-related interactive potential of such SNSs (Stromer-Galley & Foot, 2002). The researchers did not code for the Web link content, but in general, such links sent the group members to comments, Web sites, and press articles, all with a political content. This may lead younger voters to various sources of information they had not considered before, increasing their political knowledge.

One interesting aspect of the study was the overwhelming number of participants and wall post activity for Obama groups as opposed to McCain groups. This finding is congruent with expert analysis (Carr, 2008) that indicated a greater effort on Obama's campaign to appeal both to a younger group of voters and to the use of social technology. It is likely that future campaigns will develop plans to incorporate the use of SNSs into their strategy to successfully reach and utilize an active portion of the voting population. The ability to use student's social networks to discuss candidates and issues, as well as mobilize campaign efforts, gains greater significance as more Internet-savvy youth join the voting population and use the tools they are familiar with to gain access to the political process. However, we cannot establish a causal relationship for what triggered this high membership and online participation for one of the candidates. We can suggest that if one candidate is preferred by this demographic group, then young voters will use the medium that they feel more comfortable with to mobilize supporters and promote involvement.

Our analysis revealed interesting differences in short-term and long-term influences across election seasons and candidates. Obama groups during the primary season were more focused on the short-term influences, policy issues, and candidate image, whereas McCain groups were more focused on the long-term influences, partisanship, and group associations. The focus on short-term influences, at least in the Obama groups, corroborates Lipsitz et al.'s (2005) findings that voters want to learn about policy issues and candidate image during a political campaign. Linking this result to the 2008 presidential election scenario, the focus on short-term influences is not surprising when one considers the long and debated aspect of the democratic nomination. In 2007, Hillary Clinton was perceived as favorite in the nomination race, whereas Obama, although described as "smart," "charismatic," and "articulate," lacked, at first, the experience of a prolonged and highly demanding contest (Balz & Johnson, 2009). For about a year, since June 2007, when first Obama groups appeared in our sample, until June 2008, when Clinton finally endorsed Obama's democratic nomination, wall post content focused on contrasting candidates' images and experiences. At the same time, much of the discussion in the press during the campaigns pointed to Obama's "celebrity" status. Kellner (2009) suggested that Obama's ultimate success in winning the presidency was in part due to his ability to capitalize on the media spectacle that characterizes modern news coverage of politics. In a media environment like the one Kellner described, where the lines between news and entertainment are blurred, Obama's image as young, intelligent, and refreshingly different from the widely unpopular George W. Bush presidency were a strong selling point for Obama supporters. In contrast, much of the McCain campaign, particularly during the primary season, was focused on winning over the Republican Party base that was skeptical of the admittedly moderate candidate (Smerecnik & Dionisopoulos, 2009). This led to a focus on the long-term influences of the Michigan Model, partisanship, and group association. On the other hand, during the general election season, both Obama's and McCain's groups showed a balance of focus on short-term and long-term influences.

Finally, the overall positive tone of wall comments corroborates extant research (Ancu & Cozma, 2009; Postelnicu & Cozma, 2007b; Sweetser & Lariscy, 2008) that suggests comments on SNSs are usually positive and civil. However, when the analysis is broken down by candidate's mentions, a great percentage of negative comments regarding the opponent's image and policies were observed. This finding indicates that Facebook is used as venue where supporters can organize on a local level and exhibit their support for their candidate as well as frustrations they have with the opposing candidate.

The overall findings of this study bode well for the potential of Facebook and similar SNSs to foster future political civic engagement among young voters. As previous research has shown (Stromer-Galley & Foot, 2002), young people seem to find themselves naturally at home in an online environment and are particularly attracted to social media and the opportunity to contribute to the digital body of knowledge. Therefore, the effectiveness of SNSs as a forum for political activity, coupled with their natural appeal to youth, make them an optimal channel to breed political civic engagement among young voters. Furthermore, as political candidates design their campaigns, the implementation of SNSs as a campaign strategy should take center stage to reach and communicate with these young voters. More specifically, candidates and their campaign teams should take into consideration the types of discussions that these young voters are conducting to fully understand them and get their support.

Limitations and Future Research

One limitation of this study was that the sample size for Obama and McCain groups was different. This may have led to misrepresentation of McCain groups in the analysis as the overall sample was unbalanced. Although the sample size may have caused methodological and statistical shortcomings, the analysis of user-generated content does not afford the opportunity of a balanced sample. Because user-generated content is by definition generated by the user, the researchers had no control over how many people would join each candidate group or how many posts would be written during the period analyzed. This "unbalance," therefore, might reveal the very nature (i.e., wall post activity, membership) of each candidate group.

Second, when coding for the *group affiliation* category of the Michigan Model, it is possible that the very fact that the Facebook groups were organized by and for students demonstrated implicit, latent evidence of group affiliation that was not recognized in the analysis. Coding for group preference in a way that recognized this implicit affiliation (i.e., students) may have demonstrated stronger support for this category of the Michigan Model.

The use of Facebook groups as a tool for political participation is a recent phenomenon and offers many opportunities for further research. This study looked at student Facebook groups from the largest land-grant universities in battleground states and showed that political conversations dominate among young, highly educated participants. Additional research is required to suggest that online social networks facilitate political involvement among young voters in general. Future studies may find that including more universities and states can provide a broader look at how Facebook is being used by students in elections. Another interesting avenue of research would be to study whether this young population that is highly connected to the Internet and SNSs carries this behavior over the years. In other words, will these young adults continue to use the Internet and SNSs for political involvement when they grow older? Future research may also look to move outside of the student category to see how Facebook groups were used in the election among all participants. This may include the presidential candidates' main Facebook groups as well as state groups that were not limited to students. In addition, scholars may look to investigate the motivations for posting to a SNS political group by conducting in-depth interviews, focus groups, or surveys.

ACKNOWLEDGMENTS

The first two authors contributed equally to this article. We thank Dr. Lynda L. Kaid for her many helpful comments. The help of the editor and the two anonymous reviewers was also greatly appreciated.

REFERENCES

Ancu, M., & Cozma, R. (2009). MySpace politics: Uses and gratifications of befriending candidates. *Journal of Broadcasting & Electronic Media, 53*, 567–583.

Balz, D. J., & Johnson, H. (2009). *The battle for America, 2008: The story of an extraordinary election.* New York: Viking.

Bartels, L. (2000). Partisanship and voting behavior, 1952–1996. *American Journal of Political Science, 44*, 35–50.

Boyd, R. W. (1972). Popular control of public policy: A normal vote analysis of the 1968 election. *The American Political Science Review, 66*, 429–449.

Campbell, A. (1960). Surge and decline: A study of electoral change. *The Public Opinion Quarterly, 24*, 397–449.

Campbell, A., Converse, P. E., Miller, W. E., & Stokes, D. E. (1964). *The American voter. An abridgment.* New York: Wiley.

Campbell, J. E. (2008). An exceptional election: Performance, values, and crisis in the 2008 presidential election. *The Forum, 6*(4), Article 7. Retrieved from http://www.bepress.com/forum/vol6/iss4/art7/

Carr, D. (2008, November 9). The media equation: How Obama tapped into social networks' power. *New York Times.* Retrieved April 28, 2009, from http://www.nytimes.com/2008/11/10/business/media/10carr.html

CIRCLE. (2008). *Turnout by education, race and gender and other 2008 youth voting statistics.* Medford, MA: Author. Retrieved May 12, 2010, from http://www.civicyouth.org/?p=324

CNN Electoral map calculator: Election Center 2008 from CNN.com. (2008). Retrieved October 28, 2008, from http://www.cnn.com/ELECTION/2008/calculator/

The electoral map: Key states—Election guide 2008—*The New York Times*. (2008). Retrieved October 28, 2008, from http://elections.nytimes.com/2008/president/whos-ahead/key-states/map.html?scp=1&sq=electoral%20map%20key%20states&st=cse

Endres, D., & Warnick, B. (2004). Text-based interactivity in candidate campaign web sites: A case study from the 2002 elections. *Western Journal of Communication, 68*, 322–342.

Freelon, D. (2008). *ReCal: Reliability calculation for the masses*. Retrieved May 15, 2010, from http://dfreelon.org/utils/recalfront/

Iyengar, S., & Jackman, S. (2004, December). *Technology and politics: Incentives for youth participation* (CIRCLE Working Paper 24). College Park: University of Maryland, School of Public Policy, The Center for Information and Research on Civic Learning and Engagement.

Joslyn, R. (1980). The content of political spot ads. *Journalism Quarterly, 57*, 92–94.

Kaid, L. L., McKinney, M. S., & Tedesco, J. C. (2000). *Civic dialogue in the 1996 presidential campaign: Candidate, media, and public voices*. Cresskill, NJ: Hampton.

Kanel, J. V., & Quinley, H. (2008). *Exit polls: Obama wins big among young, minority voters*. CNN.com. Retrieved May 15, 2010, from http://www.cnn.com/2008/POLITICS/11/04/exit.polls

Keeter, S., Horowitz, J., & Tyson, A. (2008, November 12). *Young voters in the 2008 election*. Washington, DC: Pew Research Center for The People & The Press. Retrieved April 23, 2009, from http://pewresearch.org/pubs/1031/young-voters-in-the-2008-election

Kellner, D. (2009). Barack Obama and celebrity spectacle. *International Journal of Communication, 3*, 715–741.

Levine, P., & Lopez, M. H. (2002, September). *Youth voter turnout has declined, by any measure*. College Park: University of Maryland, School of Public Affairs, The Center for Information and Research on Civic Learning and Engagement.

Lipsitz, K., Trost, C., Grossmann, M., & Sides, J. (2005). What voters want from political campaign communication. *Political Communication, 22*, 337–354.

Martinez, M. D. (2009). *Battleground voters: Issues, race, and retrospective evaluations in Florida 2008*. Paper presented at the Annual Meeting of the Southern Political Science Association, New Orleans, January 2009.

McCain vs. Obama: The campaigning just got virtual. (2008, October 8). *The Independent*. Retrieved April 28, 2009, from http://www.independent.co.uk/life-style/gadgets-and-tech/mccain-vs-obama-the-campaigning-just-got-virtual-954386.html

Postelnicu, M., & Cozma, R. (2007a). *From MySpace friends to voters: campaigning strategies on MySpace during the 2006 U.S. congressional elections*. Paper presented at the National Communication Association Conference, Chicago, November 2007.

Postelnicu, M., & Cozma, R. (2007b). *Social network politics: A content analysis of MySpace profiles of political candidates from the 2006 US mid-terms*. Paper presented at the National Communication Association Conference, Chicago, November 2007.

Rheingold, H. (2008). Using participatory media and public voice to encourage civic engagement. In W. L. Bennett (Ed.), *Civic life online: Learning how digital media can engage youth* (pp. 97–118). Cambridge: Massachusetts Institute of Technology.

Shah, D. V., Cho, J., Nah, S., Gotlieb, M. R., Hwang, H., Lee, N., et al. (2007). Campaign ads, online messaging, and participation: Extending the communication mediation model. *Journal of Communication, 57*, 676–703.

Smerecnik, K. R., & Dionisopoulos, G. N. (2009). McCain's issue framing in 2008: The environment as freedom and a commodity. In R. E. Denton (Ed.), *The 2008 presidential campaign* (pp. 148–169). Lanham, MD: Roman & Littlefield.

Stromer-Galley, J. (2000). Online interaction and why candidates avoid it. *Journal of Communication, 50*, 111–132.

Stromer-Galley, J., & Foot, K. (2002). Citizens' perceptions of online interactivity and implications for political campaign communication. *Journal of Computed Mediated Communication, 8*(1). Retrieved from http://jcmc.indiana.edu/vol8/issue1/stromerandfoot.html

Sweetser, K. D., & Lariscy, R. W. (2008). Candidates make good friends: An analysis of candidates' uses of Facebook. *International Journal of Strategic Communication, 2,* 175–198.

Trammell, S. K. D. (2007). Candidate Campaign Blogs: Directly reaching out to the Youth Vote. *American Behavioral Scientist, 50,* 1255–1263.

Tufte, E. (1975). Determinants of the outcomes of midterm congressional elections. *The American Political Science Review, 69,* 812–826.

2008 Political landscape map: Full coverage of presidential, congressional, and gubernatorial races. (2008). Retrieved October 28, 2008 from http://www.washingtonpost.com/wp-srv/politics/interactives/campaign08/

Wells, S. D., & Dudash, E. A. (2007). Wha'd'ya know?: Examining young voters' political information and efficacy in the 2004 election. *American Behavioral Scientist, 50,* 1280–1289.

Williams, C. B., & Gulati, G. J. (2007). *Social networks in political campaigns: Facebook and the 2006 midterm elections.* Paper presented at the American Political Science Association Conference, Chicago, IL.

Index

Page numbers in *Italics* represent tables.

activation 33
activist groups: agenda setting 12–13
advertisements: Bush 10, 12; Kerry 10
advocacy groups 83
advocacy networks 12
affective attributes 9, 10; Obama ads *22*;
    YouTube ads *21*
agenda setting 5, 87; activist groups 12–
    13; political advertising 11–12; theory
    8, *see also* inter-media agenda setting
The American Voter (Campbell *et al*)
    105
Andrews, K.T. 12
anonymity 87
Anslin, E.W. 35
antisocial Internet behaviour 86
AOL 59
apathy 103
Aregbe, Farouk Olu 81
Atkin, C. 11
attribute salience 25; transfer of 9
audience activity 46

Banning, S.A. 96
Beta Coefficients: summary *43*
Biden, Joe 111
Blog for America 2
blogging 35, 58
blogs 3, 37, 102; description 59; online
    expression 71
Bortree, D.S. 83
Bowers, T.A. 11
Boyd, D.M. 3
Boyle, T.P. 11–12
Bruns, A. 3, 58
bumper stickers 2

Bush, George W. 83, 84, 119;
    advertisements 10, 12

C-SPAN 38
campaign design 119
campaign events 107; live streaming 61
campaign issues 116
campaign products 118
campaign web sites 83
Campbell, A. 37, 105, 106, 113
candidate agenda: setting 26–7
Candidate Focus 91
candidate image 106, 110, 116
candidate-to-voter interactions 104
candidate's appeal 106
candidate's image 107
Carpenter, R.C. 12
celebrity 119
chance control 39
Chapel Hill study 9
Chaudhary, Nita 14
Cho, J. 35
civic engagement 34, 102–3, 117, 119–20
civic messaging: interactive 58, 61
civic participation 47, 106
Clinton, Hillary 109, 112, 113, 119
Clinton/Lewinsky scandal 10
CNN 80, 108; Electoral Map Calculator
    108; political expression 60
Cohen, Bernard C. 8
Coleman, R. 13
college students: decision making 55–81
college students survey: conclusion 72–
    3; discussion 68–71; limitations 71–2;
    measures 63–5; method 62–3; online
    expression 71; political Internet
    activity *66*; political self-efficacy 65,
    67; results 67–8; sample demographics
    66; situational political involvement

65–7; social media 69–70; traditional Internet sources 68–9
Colorado 108
Colorado State University 108
communication 85
community building 82
computer-mediates communication (CMC) 85, 86
convenient information seeking 41
conversion 33
Correa, T. 59
Cozma, R. 107
criticism 117
cynicism: definition 35, *see also* political cynicism
Czech Republic 12

Dean, Howard 2
decision making: learning 57
decision making variables 57
democracy: Internet 60, 68
democratization myth 61
democratizing medium: Internet 60, 68
Democrats 96
discussion boards 86
donations: online 60
Downing Street Memo controversy 13

e-mail exchange 58
economy 19
education 19
Edwards, B. 12
elaboration 46; political cynicism 41–2
'Election Pulse' 84
election seasons: analyses of differences *114*
Ellison, N.B. 3
emotional expressions 113
entertaining arousal 41
entertainment 102
environment 19
European Union 12
Eveland, W.P. Jr. 38

face-to-face communication 85
Facebook 34, 44; Barack Obama affiliated groups 88; John McCain affiliated groups 88; launch of 82; McCain 3; online expression 71; political content 69; political expression 60; political profiles 102; US midterm elections 102; users 80
Facebook election: conclusions and future research 97; content categories 90; discussion 94–7; introduction 1–2; limitations 96–7; membership, activity level *93*; method 88–92; new media and the 2008 election campaign 3–5; rationale and research questions 87–8; research questions 88; results 92–4; sample 89; social media 96; variable creation 90–2
Facebook groups: building community while campaigning 82–3; differences between Obama and McCain sites *115*; effects of political messages 86–7; literature review 82–7; politics 83–5; types 82; US presidential elections (2008) 81; uses 82–3
Facebook groups study: discussion 117–21; method 108–12; results 112–17; sample characteristics *112*; theoretical background 104–7
false consensus effect 87
financial crisis 106
first-level agenda-setting effects 24
flaming 86
Flanagin, A. 86
Flickr 2
Florida 108; 2008 election 107
Florida University 108, 111
Fortman, K.K.J. 35
'friends' 102
friendship maintenance 34
fundraising speeches 2

gainful companionship 41; motivation 45
Galloway, J. 11
Gallup poll: McCain 106
gender: cynicism 48
Ghorpade, S. 11
Golan, G.J. 10–11, 25
Google 80
Google Videos 44
got out the vote (GOTV) 2
grass roots campaigning 96
gratifications 33; uses 33
group activities 118
group affiliation 116, 119; party identification 115
group associations 105, 119
Gulati, G. 84
Gurin, G. 37

Hayes, A.F. 90
Heald, G. 11
health care 19

Helms, Jesse 11
Hicks, B. 12
Holtsi, O. 17
Holzer, B. 12
Hungary 12
Hunt, Jim 11
Hwang, H. 35

Indiana 108
inflammatory conversation 81
infobyte 2
information seeking 58
instant messaging 59
intentionality 49
interactive civic messaging 58
interactivity: importance of 62
intermedia agenda setting: compelling-
    arguments hypothesis 10–11; content
    and coding 16–17; data analysis
    strategy 18; discussion 23–4; first and
    second level 8–9; first-level agenda-
    setting effects 24; hypotheses and
    research questions 14–15; intercoder
    reliability 17; introduction 7–8;
    limitations and future research 26–7;
    results 18–23; sample selection 15–16;
    theoretical contributions 25–6
internal control 39
Internet: American usage rates 59;
    democracy 60, 68; democratizing
    medium 60, 68; political self-efficacy
    61; politics 59; popularity of 34;
    public adoption 73
interpersonal communication:
    importance of 47
interpersonal motive: cynicism 47
Iraq war 9, 18, 19
issue frequencies: *The Nation 19*;
    YouTube advertising *18*
issue salience: online advertising
    agendas *20*

Kaid, L. 35, 36, 83
Katz, E.J. 58
Kee, K.F. 82
Kellner, N. 119
Kerry, John 83, 84; advertisements 10,
    12
Kim, A.E. 13
Kiousis, S. 5, 10
Krippendorf, K. 90
Kushin, Matthew 3, 4

Lariscy, R. 83

Lee, K.M. 35
Levenson 12 item index 39
Likert scale 64, 65
Limperos, Anthony 4
LinkedIn 3, 34, 44
Lipsitz, K. 119
literature review: Facebook Groups 82–
    7
live streaming: campaign events 61
lobbying 12
long-term loyalties 106
Lopez-Escobar, E. 11

McCain, John 11–12, 87–90, 96–104,
    110–14, 116–17, 119–30; anti-McCain
    Facebook groups 95; Facebook
    groups 88, 90, 111; Gallup lead 106;
    positive and negative references *94*
McCombs, M.E. 9, 11, 13
McNemar tests 93
Mann-Whitney U-tests 92
Martinez, M.D. 107
Mass Communication & Society 1
media: motivation for using 38
media salience 10
mediated political transmissions 84
Mehrabian's Conservatism-Liberalism
    scale 40
message discipline 2
Michigan Model 105, 106, 110, 116, 119
micro-blogs 3
Miller, G.W. 37
minority voters 37
Missouri 108
Missouri University 81, 108
mobilization 34, 102
mobilizing supporters 118
motives 36; primary factor loadings *42–
    3*
MoveOn.org 3; 'Obama in 30 Seconds'
    5, 7–27
Mozilla Firefox Web browser 89
MSN 69
MySpace 34, 44; Obama's page 1, 2;
    political profiles 102

The Nation 5, 16, 19, 20, 23; issue
    frequencies *19*
National Review 16
negative advertising 9; Obama 5
negative campaigning 95, 114
Nevada 108
Nevada University 108
new media: 2008 election campaign 3–5

New York Times 108; 'General Petraeus or General Betray Us' 14
Nigeria: Royal Dutch/Shell 12
North Carolina 11, 108
North Carolina State University 108, 111

Obama ads: affective attributes frequencies *22*
Obama, Barack: backing from MoveOn.org 14; descriptions 119; Facebook groups 80–1, 88–97, 102–20; high site activity 114; image 119; MySpace page 1, 2; 'Obama in 30 Seconds' (MoveOn.org) 5, 7–27; online ads 8; positive and negative references *94*; SNS integration 105; social media use 32, 87; youth voters 104
Obamacan 14
object agendas 25
object salience: transfer of 9
Ohio 108
Ohio State University 108, 111, 114, 117
Oliver, Mary 4
on-demand content 32
online advertising agendas: issue salience *20*
online communities 82
online community: real community 117
online discussion forums 3
online expression: political self-efficacy 71; politics 60
online expression index 65
online impression formation: impact of Web 2.0 technologies 85–6
online political activists: young new consumers 13–14
online political communication 102
online SNS 34
Online Social-Interactive Media (OSIM) 3
opinion leadership 49
O'Sullivan, P. 86

paid media 2
Palin, Sarah 111, 117
Papacharissi, Z. 86
Park, N. 82
partisan allegiance 105
partisan decline thesis 106
partisanship 4, 107, 119; voter choice 116
party affiliation 110
party allegiance 106

party identification: group affiliation 115
pass time 41
Pere, E.M. 38, 41
Perse and Rubin five-item elaboration scale 41
personal identities 34
Petraeus, General David 14
Pew Internet and American Life Project 13, 70
Pinkleton and Austin cynicism scale 44
Pinkleton, B.E. 35, 44
Poland 12
polarization 106
polarization of politics: social media 96
policy issues 106
political action: social networking 81
political activist advertising 12
political activist group: Web-based 26
political activity online: types of 58–60
political advertising 8, 83; agenda setting 11–12
political blogs 38
political candidate groups: official and user-generated 84
political civic engagement: fostering 119
political communication: core objectives 8
political cynicism 4, 35–6; discussion 45–50; elaboration 38, 41–2; gender 48; implications 46–9; influence of family and friends 37–8, 40–1; interpersonal motive 47; introduction 32–3; limitations and future research 49–50; literature review 33–9; locus of control 37; measurement 39–40; methods 39–44; motives 38; negative predictor 35; political information 33–4; political orientation 37, 40; political self-efficacy 37, 46; predicting 45; research questions 38–9; results 44–5; sample 39; self efficacy 40; social networks and politics 34–5; uses and gratifications 36–7; YouTube 48
political decision making: efficacy and involvement 57–8; Internet 60–2
political discussion boards 86
political efficacy 5, 56
political evaluation 41
political Internet activity: analysis *66*
political involvement: cognition 72
political knowledge 117; acquiring 107
political messages: Facebook groups 86–7

political self-efficacy 57; college students survey 65; cynicism 46; Internet 61; online expression 71; predicting *67*
political socialization 37, 47
political surveillance 34
political utility: literature 56
politics: Facebook Groups 83–5; Internet 59; online expression 60; social media 59–61
positive campaigns 95
Postelnicu, M. 83, 107
Pralle, S. 13
primary group associations 105
produsage 3, 58
profane messages 90
profanity 81
public opinion: role of news media 9
public salience 10
Purdue University 108

race: negativity 81; support for Obama 103
race-related language 95
radio: political talk 37
radio ads 2
Ragas, Matthew 5
ReCal 111
reinforcement 33
religion 93
Republic (Sunstein) 96
Republicans 96; partisanship 116
Roberts, M. 11
Royal Dutch/Shell: Nigeria 12
Rubin, A.M. 41

salience 10; of issues 19
scepticism 35
Schiffer, A.J. 13
Schoenbach, K. 10
Scott, W.A. 17
Scott's Pi 111
second-level agenda-setting effects 25
Segvic, I. 10
self expression 41
self-efficacy: low 49
Seltzer, T. 83
Semetko, H.A. 10
Shah, D. 35, 58
sharing 58
Shaw, D.L. 9
situational political involvement 57; predicting *67*
social activist groups 2, 25
social capital 56

social cognitive theory 57
social information processing theory 85
social interaction 34
social media: college students survey 69–70; definitions 59; evolving 71; motives for using 41; political cynicism 33; politics 59–61; public adoption 73; relative influence 50
social media and politics: hypotheses 62
social media use: amount of 44
social networking: political action 81
social networking sites (SNS) 3; cynicism 47; on demand 36
socialization 72
societal inequalities 37
South Korea 13
Spain 11
Spearman's rho correlations 18
stereotypes 81
substantive attributes 9
Sunstein, Cass: *Republic* 96
Sutherland, M. 11
Sweetser, K. 12, 36, 83
swing states 108

taxes 19
television 34; prime-time 81
television news 37
texting 2, 26
Twitter 2; description 59; online expression 71; political content 69; political expression 60

unintended encounters 70
union endorsements 2
US midterm Congressional elections (2006) 83, 102
US presidential election (1968) 9
US presidential election (1996) 12
US presidential election (2004) 12, 102
US presidential election (2008): Facebook groups 81; rate of Internet usage 60; rate of SNS usage 60
user communities 34
user-generated political groups 84–5
uses: gratifications 33

Valenzuela, S. 82
video games 81
video sharing 3, 34, 44
viral media 94
virtual sit-ins 13
visbyte 2
voter choice: partisanship 116

voter cynicism 33
voter turnout 96
voter-to-candidate conversations 107
voter-to-voter conversations 104
voter-to-voter integration 117
voting behaviour 106
voting intent 57
vulgarity 81

wall posts: candidates mentioned *116*
Wall Street meltdown crisis 106
Wang, S. 58
Washington Post 108
Web 2.0 Internet networks 59
Web 2.0 modalities 80
Web link 109
Weblogs 37
The Weekly Standard 16
Westling, M. 83
Wilcoxon tests 93
Williams, C. 84
Woolley, Julia 4

Yahoo! 59, 69
Yamamoto, Masahiro 3, 4
Yioutas, J. 10
young minority voters 37
young new consumers: online political
   activists 13–14
young voters: Obama 104
youth communities: online 113
youth political environment: SNS 104
youth vote 117
youth voters 103
YouTube 2, 4, 14, 34; connective
   properties 47; cynicism 48; description
   59; official campaign advertising 5;
   online expression 71; political content
   69; political expression 60; popularity
   44
YouTube advertising: affective attributes
   frequencies *21*; issue frequencies *18*